Impunity
An Ethical Perspective

# Impunity:
# An Ethical Perspective

## Six Case Studies
## from Latin America

*Edited by*
Charles Harper

WCC Publications, Geneva

Cover design: Rob Lucas

**Cover photograph:** *La Bocca della Verità*
The Mouth of Truth is a sculpture from the fourth century B.C. displayed in
the portico of the Church of Santa Maria in Cosmedin in Rome. It weighs
over a ton and measures 1,6 metres in diametre. The massive face resembling
the sun represents the Roman god Faunus, protector of nature and of fertility,
of herds, of the harvest, of game and fish - in other words, the guarantor
of the full enjoyment of basic human rights. The *Bocca della Verità* became
early on a symbol of truth and honesty: vows which were made and had to
be honoured, by rulers and the ruled. Legend has it that those who told
the truth could confidently place their hand deep into its mouth. The hand
of a liar, however, would be crushed by the awesome stone jaws. It may
be coincidental that next to the *Piazza* of the same name stood the formidable
classical prison and place of execution known as the *Doliola*.

ISBN 2-8254-1203-1

Printed in the Netherlands

# TABLE OF CONTENTS

# FOREWORD

## *Dwain C. Epps*

The recent fratricidal war in Bosnia-Herzegovina and the genocide in Rwanda illustrate in the most dramatic way the consequences of impunity. The failure in both cases to tell the truth about past wars and to try the authors of earlier atrocities for their crimes against humanity has proved once again the truth of Santayana's dictum that those who ignore the lessons of history are destined to repeat them.

Many countries around the world that were ruled by dictatorial regimes in past decades have now made the transition to limited democracies. Most of these however remain fragile, due in large part to their difficulties in dealing with the legacies of their recent past.

Their peoples all cry out for justice, for the truth to be told. Without this, there can be no national reconciliation, no real democracy, no solid basis on which to reconstruct society.

This volume, published in connection with the continuing work of the World Council of Churches on issues of impunity, shows how churches and human rights organizations in six Latin American countries struggle with these dilemmas in their societies.

These deeply moving stories and analytical studies have been gathered as a resource for people in other regions facing similar social, political and pastoral challenges. Their publication also constitutes an invitation to churches and ecumenical groups around the world to share their own experiences and the lessons they have learned with the World Council of Churches.

This is a work in progress. Concerted international action is required to improve existing international standards on impunity and to elaborate new, more effective judicial norms and instruments in response to the cry of the peoples: *Nunca Más*, Never Again!

Special thanks are due the editor of this volume, Charles Harper. As Director of the WCC's Human Rights Resources Programme for Latin America from 1973 to 1992, he was involved closely with the ministries and advocacy of the authors whose contributions he has gathered. His insightful introduction is a reflection of his deep and widely appreciated commitment to the churches and peoples of the region during some of the darkest years of their nations' history.

# FROM IMPUNITY TO RECONCILIATION

### *Charles Harper*

## Introduction

For those who follow daily news events, impunity is an inescapable topic.

Bosnian Serb leaders openly defy arrest and trial against charges that they ordered the massacre of thousands of Bosnian Muslims. The international tribunal created to try them and other alleged war criminals from former Yugoslavia is shown to be nearly powerless.

The international tribunal set up in Arusha by the United Nations' Security Council to try those responsible for the Rwandan genocide, crippled with lack of money and uncertainty of purpose, is under intense pressure from victims and their families for justice.

In South Africa, officials of the Truth and Reconciliation Commission[1] led by Anglican Archbishop Desmond Tutu travel from city to town hearing testimonies and documenting crimes committed under the brutal apartheid regime. Powerless to prosecute or punish, the Truth Commission offers leniency to those who come forward voluntarily to acknowledge their crimes and to cooperate with further investigation. Observers wonder, however, whether justice can be applied swifly enough to forestall even more outbreaks of popular outrage.

The Government of Japan is challenged – 50 years after the fact – to acknowledge having pressed 200,000 Korean, other Asian and Dutch women into sexual slavery for the benefit of troops of the Imperial Army during the Second World War. Refusing easy "pay-offs" these women, many now in their seventies, and their families, relentlessly demand from the government a public admission of guilt and an official apology.

In Seoul two former military dictators, Chun Doo Hwan and Roh Tae Woo, face charges ranging from gross corruption to murder. The chief executive officers of industries in Korea fight pitched legal battles to counter accusations of having financed these policies. Students demonstrate again in Kwangju demanding justice for their peers massacred under military orders a decade ago. The sequels of the Second World War continue to be felt in painfully sensitive ways. Fresh commemorations of the Holocaust and recurring awareness of its significance stirs introspection in Germany and elsewhere in Europe. In Italy, Nazi war criminal Erich Priebke is tried, fifty-two years later, for the massacre in 1944 of 335 Italian citizens in the Ardeantine Caves near Rome.

The Armenian *diaspora* remembers the anniversary of the genocide committed against the nation over seventy years ago, in present-day Turkey. Descendants continue to insist on international recognition of the crime committed.

People are refusing to allow history to be silenced. Succeeding generations refuse impunity and demand moral accountability for past criminal acts and a modicum of justice to ensure it.

## Impunity is a pivotal question, but what is it?

This is hardly a word which is universally understood. Until fairly recently it was an obscure concept discussed almost exclusively among lawyers and jurists.

A working definition for the purposes of this volume might run as follows: Impunity is the means by which persons accused of crimes against humanity escape being charged, tried and punished for criminal acts committed with official sanction in time of war or dictatorial rule. Impunity can be achieved through amnesty laws passed or decreed by governments under whose authority the crimes were committed or by a successive government. It can result from presidential pardons given convicted criminals who thus remain unpunished. Impunity can also occur by default – the deliberate lack of any action at all.

Another approach, described by the author of one of the studies published here, is the working definition used by the United Nations: Impunity covers those measures and practices whereby states fail in their obligation to investigate, try and sentence those responsible for the systematic practice of gross violations of human rights, and thereby impede the enjoyment by victims and their families of the right to know the truth and have their rights restored. The reasons for this failure may be a lack of political will or insufficient power to impose the rule of law upon powerful offending sectors of society, like the armed forces.

Two other contributors here remind us that "amnesty" is derived from *amnesia*, a medical term indicating the loss of memory, or forgetting. For them, impunity is often a form of political expediency, applied by those who would rather that society not dwell upon its past too closely.

As the examples above show, people around the world are standing up for the truth, demanding justice and refusing to allow history to be silenced. International symposia are being organized in many regions to probe the issues more deeply, such as a significant all-NGO conference held in March of this year in Ouagadougou,[2] Burkina Faso, on impunity as the "enemy of democracy". The churches are also joining the issue and not just in the "South". The 1997 Second

European Ecumenical Assembly convened by the Conference of European Churches and the Council of European Bishops' Conferences will deal with it under the theme: "Reconciliation: Gift of God and Source of New Life".[3]

Impunity raises fundamental dilemmas in many societies. How can crimes of the past be dealt with openly and honestly, and in such a way that the truth can be seen and justice perceived as having been served? Have the victims been heard and *their* truth acknowledged? How might future generations be liberated of their fears, hatred or guilt? Justice, if it is to be effective against impunity, must be deliberate and lasting. How can nations, peoples, tribes, ethnic groups, those associated with the perpetrators of crimes, and those close to the victims of crimes, ever be reconciled if impunity prevails? A key criterion for measuring the effectiveness of combatting impunity must, therefore, address the following question: has this society become reconciled to itself and to its past to the degree that it can become whole again?

It must be admitted that the evidences of controversy, contention and anguish – indeed profound division – over the issue of impunity *versus* justice, are sufficiently universal as to place the question of impunity at the centre of public discourse.

Since 1992 the United Nations' Commission on Human Rights and its Sub-Commission on Prevention of Discrimination and Protection of Minorities have given close attention to this matter. Based on studies being completed by two experts on "impunity of perpetrators of violations of human rights,"[4] it is hoped, in spite of the sensitive political implications of any international resolution on the subject, that action will be initiated promptly by the United Nations urging, if not requiring, member states to address the issue energetically.

### Thirst for truth, hunger for justice

Women have been among the most effective protagonists, posing sharp challenges to impunity. The remarkable member associations of FEDEFAM[5], a non- governmental organization with strong affiliates throughout Latin America, have done more than almost any other movement to make the demands for justice heard. Many persons throughout Latin America, including, as we shall see in the articles that follow, members of the Christian community, insist upon an unabated struggle for justice. However, the Chilean jurist José Zalaquett, himself a former detainee and respected advocate for human rights under the brutal Pinochet regime, summed up one side of the dilemma in *The Economist* by warning that in some cases, "the best that can be done is to insist that the full truth be known, but promise only the justice which is possible".[6]

## Hemispheric repression and the churches' response

Churches in Latin America have been in the thick of these dilemmas. Some of these churches were at the heart of the human rights struggle and witnessed first-hand the terrible effects of authoritarian military-ruled regimes upon entire populations from the mid-1960s to the end of the 1980s. On the other hand, proof exists showing that some churches and their leaders remained silent in the face of well-documented atrocities, offering justification for such practices in the name of the notorious "Doctrine of National Security". The public in such countries demands acknowledgement and confessions from these church leaders. During that period, military or military-controlled civilian governments in nineteen countries of Latin America and the Caribbean[7] carried out policies which are textbook examples of institutionalized violence against those who were considered a threat to their security and to the entrenched economic interests they protected.

The role of the United States in that process was not insignificant. The authoritative American Catholic journalist and author, Penny Lernoux, wrote some time before her untimely death:

> *Americans who once shook their heads in disbelief at the idea of CIA agents overthrowing a democratically elected government were shocked into some awareness of the truth when the CIA's role in the downfall of Salvador Allende was thoroughly documented by the United States Congress. And Chile was but part of the story.[8]*

Some of the most atrocious acts of systematic and indiscriminate murder by the armed forces and security agents of these regimes were perpetrated on civilians during that time. They generated patterns of severe repression: harassment, intimidation, threats, beatings, torture, political killings, massacres, detention without trial, imprisonment, censorship, the forced disappearance of persons, and exile.[9] Among these victims were hundreds of documented cases of Christian lay men and women, clergy and members of religious orders.[10]

## The disappeared

Trustworthy estimates have indicated that some ninety-thousand persons "disappeared" during this period in a sinister drive to wipe out suspected opponents. Military regimes tried to impose oblivion, to make people forget and indeed to erase the identity, family heritage and the very existence of their victims, as well as the ideals cherished by their generation.

One example is enough to illustrate the horror of those dark years.

In Argentina over two thousand young men and women in Buenos Aires alone were murdered on orders of the State. The recent acknowledgements by military officers from the period confirmed suspicions that many of them were put into secret places of detention and later drugged, loaded into Navy helicopters and dumped from heights of up to 5,000 feet to their deaths in the sea, or the River Plate. The confessions[11] last year of Argentinian Captain Arturo Scilingo to complicity in these acts sent shock waves throughout Argentinian society and its body politic. More than 300 infants and young children of couples killed between 1976 and 1978 were taken as "war booty" and given to childless military couples. The mammoth efforts to pinpoint their whereabouts, identify them and to restore them to their rightful relatives continues to this day.[12]

Analogous stories of equal brutality but with the use of different methods could be told of military and police abuses in Uruguay, Chile, Peru, Guatemala and El Salvador during the 1970s and 1980s. The record is well substantiated thanks often to the work of ecumenical groups and the churches in these countries, which put their relatively privileged institutional strength to good use in this period. These accounts are part of the public record through the numerous reports of UN Working Groups, Special Rapporteurs and Committees.

A dramatic model of the tenacious quest for establishing the facts was provided in Brazil. A clandestine six-year research project was carried out by a group of persons, some of them former victims of the regime. Under the auspices and protection of the Roman Catholic Archdiocese of São Paulo and in close cooperation with the WCC, the team of well placed individuals secretly copied the entire files of all the military court records detailing the use of torture from 1968 to 1979. The findings were published in 1985 in the form of a popular book, *Brasil Nunca Mais*, and pioneered the series of *Nunca Más* publications in Latin America. [13]

Church groups did not only document human rights abuses. They provided what was often the only source of legal defence for prisoners, and – in the time of severe curtailment of freedom of the press and of freedom of association – became during the darkest hours of repression the "voice of the voiceless". They were able to set up tight, efficient entities, such as the MEDH in Argentina, and FASIC[14] in Chile, which sheltered and hid people sought by the military and the secret police, assisted people to escape into exile, provided professional guidance in rehabilitation of victims and supported the work of the families of the disappeared. Dozens of these groups all over the hemisphere, themselves the object of threats, suddenly brought contemporary vitality to a Gospel imperative of costly solidarity with the persecuted, offering hope to desperate people.

A significant number of these ecumenical groups are today at the forefront of the impunity struggle, precisely because of the credibility they earned from years of human rights advocacy.

## Spiritual integrity and political will

The strength of will of committed churches and human rights groups to address the issue of impunity can be gauged only in the light of their own painful history.

A lucid rendition of such a process, quite representative of the path taken by so many groups across the continent, was given by Argentinian theologian José Miguez Bonino, a past President of the WCC.

> *What have we Argentinians learned from our experience? That human rights constitute an indivisible unity; that the struggle for human rights, to be truly effective, must be that of a whole people and not that of a few; that to build an effective democracy three elements must be present: the ethical principle on which life itself is built on a respect for the dignity of persons, for truth and for justice; a vision of a nation which we want, to be based on justice and participation; and finally the progressive realization of this project.* ***For Christians to be involved in the struggle, what is at stake is the very authority of our faith. Because we have faith we struggle for human rights and through our struggle we witness to our faith (bold added – ed.)*** [15]

The international ecumenical family, including the World Council of Churches, became heavily involved in support of this struggle, especially from the early 1970s. At the request of member churches of the WCC, special missions[16] were sent for fact-finding and pastoral solidarity in critical situations. It provided means for sometimes secret operations to help people flee across borders. Certainly a great deal of effort went into assistance of victims of repression. Above all, however, it concentrated on strengthening the ability of newly formed teams of men and women to defend and assist new types of labour union leaders, community-based political cadres, professionals, students, and popular neighborhood youth who were determined to restore democracy and to lay down the foundations of post-military societes based on justice and participation.

The studies contained in this volume are a reflection of that work.[17]

## Official amnesty for criminal violators of human rights

Since 1990 most governments in Latin America and the Caribbean have been once again democratically elected following military rule. Nonetheless, Christian clergy, lay leaders and human rights organizations have levelled powerful criticism at governments which have succumbed to military pressure and confirmed decrees granting impunity from prosecution for crimes to many officers, security agents and their accomplices. Such amnesty laws have been passed, successively since 1979, in Chile, Brazil, Uruguay, Argentina, Guatemala, Honduras, El Salvador and Peru.

Impunity has become a central issue in most of these countries. It has become abundantly clear that it is one which will not soon go away. Out of the many hundreds of identified offenders, the names of men and places such as Argentinian Navy Captain Alfredo Astiz, Uruguay's *Libertad* Prison, Chile's General Augusto Pinochet, Guatemala's General Rios Montt, and El Salvador's Major Roberto D'Aubuisson, evoke the spectres of some of the most abhorrent, grotesque and dehumanizing experiences in the history of the hemisphere.

## Asserting ethical bases for resisting impunity

The opposition to military hegemony during the twenty-year human rights struggle in Latin America provided new leaders for what has become known as the "civil society". They are credible and influential actors in the social and political arenas. They give strength to indigenous communities, landless peasants, women's organizations and urban peace coalitions as well as to the continuing human rights movement.

They have been pressing for an end to the practice of impunity and are convinced that it is the major obstacle to the achievement of justice. Impunity prevents the full rehabilitation of victims, an authentic social reconciliation and the establishment of sustainable democracy.

The WCC has requested several such persons to reflect from an ethical perspective upon the issue of impunity. In two cases they have shared what they had written earlier. Clearly they resist impunity not only out of a deep respect for the rule of law, nor simply as the spontaneous expression of human solidarity towards those who suffer. As will be seen, they draw deliberately upon the deep well-springs of their faith and the tenets of their professional and religious ethos. Some of the authors articulate their convictions theologically. Others offer a biblical imperative, illuminating a strong respect for the law as a guarantor of social viability and human conviviality. Still others approach impunity as a major source of medical disorder. For them, impunity constitutes a barrier to the creation of a just and peaceful environment for succeeding generations. We are most grateful to them for their timely reflections.

All the studies included here probe the ethical dimensions of impunity. They have been written out of the harsh experience of protagonists in the struggles of six Latin American countries.

Other case studies might have been considered.[18] However this selection provides an excellent multi-disciplinary sample of how churches and ecumenical groups in Latin America see the issue of impunity.

## Common threads

A number of common ethical themes emerge from these studies. They appear as prerequisites for the achievement of reconciliation, in other words, wholeness for society and for its individual members.

- The importance of preserving memory
- The need for the truth to be known and told
- The need for punitive justice to be served
- The need for acknowledgment to be made
- The role of forgiveness
- The primacy of hope

## A resource for interchange

These studies have been compiled here as a resource for Christian communities around the world, as well as for people of other faiths,[19] who are wrestling with similar dilemmas related to impunity in their own countries and regions. They do not constitute a finished product. Rather, they are an open invitation extended to others to share their experiences and reflections with the World Council of Churches, which continues to address the question of impunity especially through the work of the CCIA.

## A liturgical blueprint

It is fitting to conclude this introduction on impunity with a reference to the liturgy, that act which is central for Christians and which contains within its practice the ethical norms of a reconciled community. In various forms, Christians around the world and in many cultures celebrate this act of intelligence and power. The liturgy contains within it the essential symbolic steps necessary to resist impunity and to work for reconciliation.

- The reading of the law, prominently and publicly declared, as an unambiguous criterion for social and civic behaviour.
- A call for repentance directed to those who have broken the law.

• A confession of such acts, and repentance for complicity in violence, which together open the way for dialogue between the aggressors and the aggressed.

• The proclamation of hope in "good news".

• The declaration of forgiveness, opening the way to regeneration and life in community.

• Public reconciliation, made visible and concrete in the eucharist.

An irony, but surely not an accident, of history occurred when an assassin's bullet struck down Monseñor Oscar Arnulfo Romero, the Archbishop of San Salvador and a strong advocate for justice, at the precise moment when he was celebrating the eucharistic act with his people.

The credibility of the movement to combat impunity comes down, in the final analysis, to the integrity of those persons who have risked all for new hope. As one of the authors in this book has eloquently written, martyrs carve out a physical track in history, into which we can step and walk more easily.

## NOTES

1. For an understanding of the legislative framework and aims of the Commission, see the booklet entitled *Truth and Reconciliation Commission*, published in 1994 by the Justice in Transition Institute, Rondebosch, South Africa.

2. Participants gathered under the co-sponsorship of the Commission Africaine des Droits de l'Homme et des Peuples, the Union Interafricaine des Droits de l'Homme, the Centre International des Droits de la Personne et du Développement Démocratique, the Groupe d'Étude et de Recherche sur la Démocratie et le Développement Économique et Social en Afrique, Women in Law and Development in Africa, the International Commission of Jurists and the Fédération Internationale des Droits de l'Homme. See also the consensus document, published in a quadri-lingual format, of an interdisciplinary seminar entitled *Breaking with the "Culture of Impunity" in Rwanda and Burundi* which gathered members in Geneva and Lausanne, Switzerland, of the *diaspora* of these countries, along with students, former students and members of the faculty of the Graduate Institute of Development Studies (IUED) in Geneva into what became a "Listening and Reconciliation Group for the Great African Lakes Region". Geneva: IUED, 1995.

3. Graz, Austria, 23-29 June 1997.

4. Mr. Louis Joinet (France) on "the question of the impunity of perpetrators of violations of human rights (civil and political rights)" and Mr. El Hadji Guissé (Senegal) with respect to the violations of economic, social and cultural rights. Their *interim* reports to the Subcommission on Prevention of Discrimination and Protection of Minorities of June 1995 listed as documents E/CN.4/Sub.2/1995/18 and E/CN.4/Sub.2/1995/19, respectively. The UN Commission on Human Rights at its 51st session in Geneva also requested the Working Group on arbitrary detention to examine the problem of impunity.

5. La Federación Latinoamericana de Asociaciones de Familiares de Desaparecidos.

6. *The Economist,* July 1, 1995. Zalaquett has elsewhere provided a most useful typology of situations of transition from military domination to civilian rule and of the "political constraints faced by those seeking to establish truth and justice regarding prior

human-rights abuses". They range, historically and geographically, from a) situations in which there are no significant political constraints (such as in Germany following WWII, or in Nicaragua after Somoza fled) to; b) instances where the defeated forces have lost legitimacy but retain control of the armed forces (e.g. Argentina in 1983 and Greece in 1974), to; c) where military rulers allow a civilian government to come to power, but on their own terms (Uruguay); d) one of gradual transition and popular forgiveness (Spain after Franco); e) the creation of a new coalition government in circumstances of unresolved armed conflict (e.g. the Philippines) and, finally; f) those cases where ethnic, national or religious divisions impede pacification (as occurred, he argues, in Uganda in the late 1980s). For a full discussion of these theses, developed at a 1988 seminar of "academics, lawyers, clerics and activists" around the world, see the monograph *State Crimes: Punishment or Pardon?*, distributed by the Aspen Institute, New York, 1989. Ample reference is also made to this seminar in the foreword and notes of the book by Lawrence Weschler, *A Miracle, A Universe* (cf the Bibliography in this volume.)

7. (in rough chronological order of military control): Nicaragua, Paraguay, Guatemala, Haiti, Brazil, Uruguay, Bolivia, Colombia, Chile, Argentina, El Salvador, Peru, Honduras, Panama, and the Dominican Republic and to a lesser extent in five other Spanish- or French-speaking countries.

8. In *Cry of the People*, New York: Doubleday & Company, Inc., 1980, p.157.
The responsibility of successive United States administrations in the support of Latin American repressive regimes during the past thirty years is well documented by historians and observers within the U.S. itself. For example, the 206th General Assembly (1994) of the Presbyterian Church (USA) meeting in Wichita, Kansas, June 10-17 1994, passed a resolution "On Calling for the Closure of the School of the Americas". The resolution reiterated, in particular, its concern "about policies and activities of the United States government that relate to prospects for peace in this hemisphere and throughout the world", pointing out that "graduates of the School of the Americas have been among Latin American military leaders with the worst record of human rights violations" (Letter from the Stated Clerk to Synods and Presbyteries of the PCUSA dated August 29, 1994). In this regard, the fundamental issue of the complicity of international political, economic and military interests in particular situations where crimes against humanity are perpetrated cannot be ignored in the discussion on ultimate accountability and the implementation of justice.

9. English-readers will appreciate the sobering account of the policies of repression exercised by military regimes during that period, in *Poverty and Power: Latin America After 500 Years* (Edited by George Gelber, London: CAFOD, 1992) (cf. esp. the chapter by Jenny Pearce "A Short History of Latin America").

10. *1492-1992: Prophètes pour un autre Nouveau Monde*, Paris: DIAL (Diffusion de l'information sur l'Amérique latine), 1992

11. Recorded in the Argentinian best-selling book by Horacio Verbitsky, *El Vuelo*, Buenos Aires: Ed. Planeta, 1995.

12. *Botin de Guerra*, by Julio E. Nosiglia (Buenos Aires:Cooperativa Tierra fertil Ltda., 1985) describes the remarkable work of the Grandmothers of the Plaza de Mayo, a feisty and determined group which set themselves up in 1977 to begin the search for their grandchildren.

13. The impact of this study on ordinary people in Brazil was felt to an unexpected decree. See a full and cliff-hanging description of how, "against tremendous odds", torture victims and ecumenical human-rights workers dug out the truth about the practice of torture, in the book by Lawrence Weschler, *A Miracle, A Universe: Settling Accounts with Torturers*, New York: Random House (Pantheon Books), 1990. Portuguese edition: *Um milagre, um universo: o acerto de contas com os torturadores*

(translated by Tomás Rosa Bueno). Sao Paulo: Editora Schwarcz Ltda., 1990. Please refer to the Bibliography for a full consideration of these multiple efforts to establish the facts of repression in Latin America. Mention has been made of the seminal work in Brazil. Another similar contribution has been made by members of the religious and church communities in Paraguay, which gathered and built up a careful record of repression under the 30-year regime of General Alfredo Stroessner. A formidable collection of documents and files, known as the "Archive of Terror" was uncovered in Paraguay with the overthrow of Stroessner. The contents of the archive only confirm the accuracy of the findings of church and secular human rights entities there but have unearthed the vast strategy and details of "Operation Condor", closely linked to hit squads assassination schemes targetting the opponents of the Chilean, Argentinian, Bolivian, Uruguayan and Brazilian military regimes. See the recent article by Keith M. Slack, entitled "Operation Condor and Human Rights", in Human Rights Quarterly (Baltimore: Johns Hopkins University Press), May 1996, pp. 492-506. Additional ecumenical and human rights groups in Ecuador, Haiti, Honduras, Colombia, Nicaragua, Guatemala and elsewhere in Latin America and the Caribbean regions have developed strong programmes of action-reflection in the combat against impunity.

14. Ecumenical Movement for Human Rights (MEDH), and the Social Foundation of the Christian Churches (FASIC)

15. Prof. Bonino gave a moving presentation to the meeting (1985) of WCC's Central Committee held in Buenos Aires, entitled "Human Rights: The Argentinian Experience".

16. A widely-representative ecumenical delegation went to Peru in October 1990 at the beginning of President Alberto Fujimori's tenure. Its report, *Peru and Human Rights*, as well as one written by a follow-up delegation one year later, highlighted the indispensable role of the resilient human rights entities working year-round in concert with the affected sectors of society in the defence and promotion of rights.

17. Before the coming into formal existence of the Latin America Council of Churches (CLAI), in 1982, the WCC was called to exert a significant role in equipping and strengthening the work of Christian communities in human rights ministries and mobilization, and set up a specific programme for these purposes (the Human Rights Resources Office for Latin America).

18. See the extensive appended bibliography listing other initiatives of this nature.

19. For example, an excellent consideration of one indispensable ingredient of reconciliation is developed in a recent tri-lingual (Arabic, French and English) publication entitled *Etudes sur la Tolérance*, by Abdelfattah Amor, Néji Baccouche and Mohamed Talbi. Edited by the Institut Arabe des droits de l'homme and the Académie Tunisienne "Beit Al-Hikma", Tunis, 1995.

# PERU

Peru's cruel civil war between the Shining Path (Sendero) armed insurgency and the Armed Forces wrought great destruction and caused the deaths of twenty-five thousand persons among the civilian population over a fifteen-year period (1980-1995). The practices of torture, forced disappearance and summary executions perpetrated equally by the Army, paramilitary organizations and insurgents, have affected to a preponderant degree the indigenous altiplano populations, the urban poor, the dispossessed and the vulnerable sectors of society. The militarization of the drug trade, and of official efforts undertaken to combat it, increased sharply the level of political violence in the country. Human rights workers have themselves been made deliberate targets of intimidation, death threats and repression for their investigative work and public stances against injustice.

# THE LEGALIZATION OF IMPUNITY:
# AN OBSTABLE TO NATIONAL RECONCILIATION

## *José Burneo*

*If you had been imprisoned*
*I could have delivered you*
*Had you had been ill*
*I could have healed you*
*Had you travelled*
*I could have visited you*
*Now that I see you dead*
*I cannot even lay you in the tomb[1]*

## Introduction

Over the past 20 years, an entirely new kind of legislation has been enacted in the Latin American region – legislation on impunity.[2] The purpose of this is to allow serious, massive violations of human rights, perpetrated on the whole by the Armed Forces, to go unpunished.

The powers-that-be in the countries concerned seek to justify this impunity provided for by law through an extraordinarily similar political and ideological line of reasoning, reiterated by civilian and military elites. Thus, in the last decade, a democratically elected president was heard to say, to justify such legislation : "The country needs reconciliation to face a difficult but promising future".[3]

The countries that have resorted to this strange instrument of "reconciliation" include Chile (1978), Brazil (1979), Uruguay (1986), Argentina (1983, 1986, 1987, 1989), Guatemala (1986), Honduras (1987) and El Salvador (1987, 1993)[4]. To this list must now be added the most recent case, Peru (1995), which we shall be describing in the following pages.

Considering the limited scope of this work, priority will be given to some of the key aspects of the problem of impunity. Insofar as possible, a parallel will be drawn between what occurred in Peru and the countries in the southern part of Latin America. We shall first refer to the issue of material damage, that is, the magnitude of the crimes committed; in other words, we shall describe what happened. Second, we shall take up the issue of legitimacy. Is it consistent with international law for a state to grant impunity for serious, massive violations of human rights? Third, we shall consider the effectiveness of the struggle against legalized impunity. Finally, by way of conclusion, we shall submit a few thoughts for reflection.

## I. The magnitude of the crimes committed

A brief outline of some of the historical features of Peruvian society may help to give a better understanding not only of the armed political violence or "domestic war" that began in 1980 but also the human rights violations and the fight to defend human rights.

### A. *The national context*

Peru is a country that resembles Bolivia and Ecuador more than Chile, Argentina and Uruguay which have a more homogeneous population from a racial standpoint – the indigenous component being small – and, in general, less acute poverty than in Peru. Lima, the capital of the republic, has a population of approximately seven million inhabitants; however, it is estimated that only 20% of the working population have a proper job. The remainder are unemployed and under-employed. About 11,500,000 people, that is, half the country's population, live in a state of abject poverty.[5]

Peasant mobilization and pressure, the fruit of the country's strong, historical indigenous component, brought about an Agrarian Reform (1970) – exceptional in Latin America – that has yet to take place in the southern part of the continent. There are no large land-owners left in Peru, but the Agrarian Reform solved neither the agrarian problem nor the issue of indigenous, peasant poverty. This section of the country's population thus began to migrate around the middle of this century from the countryside to the city.

Perhaps one of the greatest problems in the country, shared by other peoples on the continent, is the inevitable legacy of a long period of colonial domination. This legacy has two very clear-cut dimensions, which have been institutionalized to such an extent that they are accepted as natural, pervading the social life and order in the ex-colonial countries. One side of the legacy is the integrist model of the colonizer, perceived as setting the values which must naturally apply in the ex-colonial society. The other side is the disregard for indigenous culture and the people who created it. The marginalization of the indigenous cultural dimension, usually treated as mere folklore, is particularly striking amongst the peoples with the strongest indigenous roots in Latin America, where the mestizo and white elites have taken the place of the former colonizers. Thus, in the course of this century, any talk of racism has been late in coming in Peru.[6] "Racism stands out as an anti-democratic ideology in the history of the republic. If democracy has made such little progress in Peru since independence, some one hundred and seventy odd years ago, it is because racism has prevailed."[7]

The scant value attached to Peruvian Indians and mestizos who have Indian traits has been and is one of the characteristics of Peruvian society and state institutions. The life and basic rights of the indigenous people, or those who look like them, are those of second class citizens; they can be thwarted by individuals and state agents, particularly those in charge of repression, yet such violations cause no concern either among those perpetrating the offences or national public opinion. Thus, the death of 20 indigenous women in the Andes is less important than that of a single citizen in the capital of the republic.

### B. The "domestic war" and human rights violations

The above-mentioned points are important when it comes to understanding the magnitude and nature of the human rights violations in the country which are subsequently to be covered by the amnesty. Let us first look at the question of quantity. If we compare the case of Peru with Brazil, Chile and Uruguay, the first difference worth noting is that the number of victims in Peru exceeds the sum of those in the latter three countries put together. In Peru, taking into account the fact that it is impossible to calculate the total number of victims for various reasons, no fewer than 25,000 people had died by December, 1994,[8] as a result of the domestic armed conflict begun in April 1980 by the "Shining Path".[9] The armed forces caused approximately 46% of the deaths, the Shining Path about 48% and the MRTA some 6%.[10] Ten percent of the above-mentioned victims were law enforcement officers; that is, 90% were civilians.[11]

Over and beyond these victims, one must add the extra-judicial executions by law enforcement officers. The continuation of this practice led the United Nations Special Rapporteur on extra-judicial executions, Mr. Bacre Waly Ndiaje, to consider that impunity had been institutionalized.[12]

In this picture of horror, one must also include the practice of enforced disappearance by the Peruvian state. Peru is listed as one of the countries with the largest number of missing persons, in the annual reports of the Working Group on Enforced or Involuntary Disappearances of the United Nations Human Rights Commission. According to its last report,[13] there are 2,880 missing detainees in Peru (1982-1994); according to Amnesty International and Peruvian human rights organizations, this figure should in fact be no less than 4,000 persons.[14] According to the United Nations report,[15] the number of persons registered as detained and missing in the case of Brazil is 46 (1964-1977), 861 in Chile (1973-1976) and 3,000 in Argentina (1975-1978).

It is important to highlight at this juncture:

1) that the disappearances in Peru occurred under democratic regimes and not military dictatorships as in the three above-mentioned countries,

2) that despite the foregoing, the situation in Peru is in general more serious from a quantitative viewpoint, and

3) that the events were monitored by the United Nations Working Group on Enforced or Involuntary Disappearances.[16]

In Peru, the widespread, institutionalized practice of torturing detainees as a result of the armed conflict (and common criminals in general, which we shall not go into here) is worthy of special mention. The Committee against Torture, established under the Convention against Torture and other cruel, inhuman or degrading punishment or treatment, has stated : "The Committee is gravely concerned by a large number of complaints from both non-governmental organizations and international bodies or committees, which report a widespread practice of torture (in Peru) during investigations into terrorist acts, as well as by the impunity granted the torturers."[17]

The gigantic scale of torture can be deduced from the fact that:

1) the thousands of missing, detained persons are generally tortured to death,[18]

2) a vast majority of the thousands of persons detained as a result of the armed conflict – it is calculated that there are no fewer than 5,000 detainees at present[19] – are tortured,[20]

3) "a common form of torture against women is rape".[21]

The exile of thousands of Chileans, Argentinians, Uruguayans and even Brazilians in the past was one of the consequences of human rights violations in the countries concerned. In the case of Peru, this did not occur to the same extent; instead, it created a new kind of equally terrible exile on a huge scale. Indeed, there appear to be only two thousand Peruvians with the official status of political refugees in the world. This may partly be explained by a change in government policy in general with respect to political asylum. However, the main reason is that most Peruvians who need asylum are not people from the city, but peasants of Quechua and Andean origin who have probably never even heard of political asylum. Whence the proliferation of displaced persons within the country, the suffering of hundreds of thousands of persons who become political refugees in their own country. Yet the "displaced" are not only denied the slightest advantage enjoyed by political refugees; they are also persecuted, abandoned to their fate, suspected of infiltration by subversive elements. They are genuinely "stateless" in their own country as the state refuses to provide any identity papers.[22] It is estimated that there are between 600,000 and 800,000 internally displaced persons in Peru.[23]

The terrorist strategy and policy of the Shining Path was something new in South America. According to the statistics of the Peruvian National Coordinating Unit for Human Rights,[24] the Shining Path was responsible for approximately 12,000 deaths between 1980 and December, 1994. Noteworthy is the fact that 80% of its victims were assassinated in cold blood and not as a result of an armed conflict. The fact that over 9,000 persons, mainly civilians, from the poor sectors of society – Quechua Andean peasants or Amazonian Indians – were assassinated[25] by a political organization may explain the widespread fear that reigned among the civilian population.

### C. Towards a democratic-authoritarian state

The 1980s in Peru was a decade of violence. A series of factors came together during those years: a lengthy economic crisis reflected in mass poverty, social discontent compounded by the overall impact of modernization in the country, rampant armed and political violence, a crisis within the state and political parties. The combination of all these factors created the conditions for desperate political solutions in keeping, nonetheless, with the new world order. This was the time of "soft dictatorships" and "harsh democracies", that is, regimes combining democratic and authoritarian features.

The armed forces in Peru, as in other countries in the region, turned not only into political supporters but also inevitable, indispensable partners in building the new order; thus they also became one of its key instigators. Given the absence or obsolescence of the political parties, the ongoing armed conflict, and in order to control the social unrest caused by the economic model, the armed forces became even more necessary than before.[26]

This was also the time of "independent" political leaders and statesmen and "new parties" actively and vocally intolerant, and the era of *de facto* power. The real protagonists made up a power bloc. Alongside the armed forces were national and transnational businessmen, the World Bank and an ultra-liberal "class" of technocrats.[27] The different components of this power bloc were brought together by the shared desire for order both in the social (public order), and in the economic and political spheres. Two projects thus dovetailed neatly, one for public law and order and the other for economic order, proposed respectively by the armed forces and the IMF. The one needed the other: the first to gain legitimacy and the second to function.[28]

It is in this context that impunity was legalized in Peru; those responsible for all kinds of human rights violations during the fight against terrorism from 1980 to June 1995 were amnestied.

## II. International law and impunity

### A. *Scope of laws on impunity in Peru*

The Peruvian amnesty law No. 26479, published in the official bulletin on 15.06.95, states in article 1 : "A general amnesty shall be granted to military, police or civilian staff, whatever their military, police or state function at the time, who have been denounced, investigated, charged, tried or sentenced for common and military offences in the common or exclusively military courts, respectively, for any offences resulting from or rooted in the fight against terrorism that may have been committed individually or as a group since May 1980 until the enactment of this law".

The law grants total impunity to those who fought terrorism, covering all kinds of "common and military offences", that is, the rape and assassination of girls and women, cold-blooded murder of children and adults in collective massacres, enforced disappearances, torture, extra-judicial executions of combattants who surrendered, etc. In a nutshell, any form of atrocity, without exception, has been amnestied.

A few days later, a law supplementing the amnesty was enacted; Law No. 26492, published in the official bulletin on 02.07.95. It introduces two important new elements :

1) it extends the amnesty not only to cases in which the perpetrator "has been denounced..." (Art. 1 of law 26479, see above), but also to all cases : "irrespective of whether the military, police or civilian staff involved has been denounced or not" (Art. 3 of law 26492);

2) it provides that the amnesty granted "cannot be overthrown by the courts" (Art. 2 of law 26492); that is, it prevents the judiciary from fulfilling one of its main functions in a state where the rule of law prevails – ensuring a legal provision is consistent with the principles of law and/or legislation which takes precedence.

### B. *International law and impunity*

The violation of international law: The laws granting total impunity enacted in Peru either directly violate any number of international instruments that bind the Peruvian state, or contravene international standards of behaviour in the field of human rights. For example :

1) *The Universal Declaration of Human Rights,* which establishes, in addition to the right to life and ban on torture, that everyone has the right "to an effective remedy by the competent national tribunals" (Art. 8) and all are equal before the law (Art. 7)

2) *The International Covenant on Civil and Political Rights* which provides that the state shall undertake to ensure that any person whose rights are violated shall have an effective remedy notwithstanding that the violation has been committed by persons acting in an official capacity (Art. 2 para. 3 a); and stipulates that in the event the life of the nation is threatened, the state shall not be entitled to suspend fundamental rights (Art. 4) as the Peruvian amnesty does.

3) *The Convention against Torture and Cruel, Inhuman or Degrading Treatment,* which provides that each state party shall qualify any act of torture as an offence according to its penal legislation (Art. 4) and shall judge those who commit the offence of torture (Art. 5 and 6).

4) *Principles on the Effective Prevention of Arbitrary and Summary Extra-legal Executions,* recommended by ECOSOC in resolution 1989/65 of 24 May 1989, which reiterate the ban on extra-legal, arbitrary and summary executions it affirmed that no exceptional circumstances, whether war or otherwise, shall be invoked as a justification (Art. 1) and that a thorough, impartial investigation shall be made (Art. 9).

5) *Article 3 of the Four Geneva Conventions of August 1949 and the Additional Protocol II on the Protection of the Victims of Non-International Armed Conflicts* (Art.4) which ban attacks on the life, health and physical and mental well-being of those not involved in the armed conflict; such standards therefore apply in less serious circumstances, for example when a country like Peru does not recognize the existence of an armed, non-international conflict on its territory.

6) *Declaration of the United Nations General Assembly on the Protection of All Persons From Enforced Disappearance* (Resolution 47/133 of 18 December 1992), which specifies that no state may justify such a practice by invoking a war or other exceptional circumstances (Art. 7).

7) *American Convention on Human Rights* of the Organization of American States (OAS), which provides that states shall guarantee the right to justice, i.e. shall "respect the rights and freedoms ... of all persons subject to their jurisdiction" (Art.1, para. 1), which includes the right of all persons to be legally protected "against acts that violate their fundamental rights ... even though such violation may have been committed by persons acting in the course of their official duties" (Art.25, para.1). It likewise enshrines equality before the law (Art.24). Furthermore, in the event of war or other exceptional circumstances (Art. 27), fundamental rights shall not be suspended. Peru' s law 26479 provides, in fact, for just such a suspension as it

considers the Peruvian state to be free of any obligation in the field of human rights. By thus waiving responsibility for human rights violations on its territory, it fails to shield the victims of violations of their fundamental rights, thwarting their right to protection and access to justice.

8) *Inter-American Convention to Prevent and Sanction Torture (1985) and the Inter-American Convention on the Enforced Disappearance of Individuals (1994) (OAS)*, the first ratified by Peru and the second approved by a vote in favour, which provide that both types of violations are unjustifiable even in the event of war and similar circumstances (Art.5 and Art. 10 respectively).

The Human Rights Committee of the International Covenant on Civil and Political Rights has spoken out clearly against impunity. In the cases of Uruguay[29] and Argentina,[30] the Committee expressed concern because the laws in question contribute to an atmosphere of impunity that might undermine democratic order and weaken respect for human rights.

Finally it is worth recalling  that within the Organization of American States, OAS:

1) the Inter-American Human Rights Commission ruled, with respect to Argentina and Uruguay, that the laws on "Due Obedience" and *Punto Final* (Argentina) as well as the law on the "Expiry of the Punitive Will of the State" (Uruguay), infringe the American Declaration on Human Rights and Duties and the American Human Rights Convention.[31]

2) the Inter-American Court of Human Rights recently declared that the "enacting of a law clearly contrary to the commitments made by a State on ratifying or acceding to the Convention constitute a violation thereof and, in the event this violation affects protected rights and freedoms of given individuals, engages the international responsibility of said State".[32]

## III. The effectiveness of the struggle against the legalization of impunity

### A. *What has occurred in southern Latin America and Peru*

It may be useful to take stock of the effectiveness of the fight against the legalization of impunity in other Latin American countries in order to situate what is going on in Peru. We wish to give a very brief, panoramic view of what has occurred in the southern part of the continent.

The fight against impunity actually covers three different, though complementary, aspects. *Official recognition*, through an impartial,

thorough investigation, of the crimes committed, is the first aspect to
consider in the struggle against impunity, which is part and parcel of
the *right to truth*. Second, the *legal sanction*.[33] Lastly, *redress and
compensation* of the victims or their families.[34]

The way in which a state reacts to the three key issues it must
tackle after a period of serious, large-scale human rights violations does
not follow any pre-determined pattern. Thus, for example, the response
to the problem of recognition – that is, establishing an official report
of events, ascertaining the facts or, conversely, refusing to investigate
what occurred – does not determine the reaction to the other core
issues. In an attempt to sum up the foregoing, one can observe the
following in Peru and the countries in the southern part of the
continent:

| COUNTRY | RECOGNITION | SANCTION | REDRESS/ COMPENSATION |
|---|---|---|---|
| Argentina | Yes | No[1] | No (yes ?)[2] |
| Brazil | No | No | No (yes ?)[3] |
| Chile | Yes | No[4] | Yes |
| Uruguay | No | No | No |
| Peru | No | No | No |

1   The condemned leaders of the Military Junta were pardoned. No one is today in prison for past
     abuses.
2   The law on redress is very recent (January 1995) and no one knows how it will be applied.
3   The law on redress is also very recent (August 1995) and its implementation will have to be
     assessed at a later date.
4   There has only been one exception in fact to the law on impunity in Chile – the judging of the
     two perpetrators of the crime against Orlando Letelier in Washington (1976); this was a means
     of avoiding extradition, as requested by the United States.

### B. The Peruvian judiciary and the legalization of impunity in Peru

The day after the first law on impunity was officially published,
Judge Antonia Saquicuray, a woman of outstanding calibre and
courage, took up the challenge. It was public knowledge that the
government and its overwhelming parliamentary majority wished to
paralyze the penal proceedings begun two months previously by the
Judge for the collective assassination of fourteen adults and a ten year
old child ("Barrios Altos" massacre, Lima, November 1991). The case
was against Army General Julio Salazar Monroe, former head of the

National Intelligence Service, and other officers in the same section.[35]

The decision handed down by the judge on 16 June 1995 ruled that: "article one of Law 26479 was inapplicable" as it violated the American Human Rights Convention (Art. 1.1, Art. 8.1 and Art. 25.1) and the political constitution of Peru, and ordered "that the proceedings underway be pursued".

The authors of the law, and the senior military command involved, were amazed at the judge's courage. This was not part of their plans. The counter-attack took place on various levels. First, "anonymous" death threats.[36] Then, threats of penal proceedings for "misinterpreting" the law.[37] Third, the enactment a few days later (July 2), of a second law on impunity, "interpreting" the first, in order to ensure that the Supreme Court of Justice would overturn the judge's ruling.[38]

The Supreme Court of Justice ruled along the lines sought by the government-military command alliance. The Court: a) declared the Judge's decision null and void; b) ordered the unrestricted freedom for the military denounced; c) ordered the Judicial Supervisory Body "to determine the reponsibility, where appropriate" of the Judge who had dared to refuse to apply the law on impunity. This latter measure was and is a threat to any judge who dares in future to follow the example of Judge Antonia Saquicuray.

It is important at this juncture briefly to highlight the basic elements of the arguments put forward by the Peruvian Supreme Court of Justice. The Court affirms that:

1) the state is entitled to grant amnesties without any limitations whatsoever, that is, for all types of offences including those that can be described as lèse-humanité or crimes against humanity;[39]

2) the international treaties binding the state, in this case in the field of human rights, do not bind the Congress of the Republic, which is sovereign, and therefore brooks no limitations on the exercise of its legislative powers.[40]

The position adopted by the Peruvian Supreme Court of Justice reflects an impardonable ignorance of the development of international law[41] after the Second World War, beginning with the International Military Court at Nuremberg.[42]

### C. Has impunity triumphed among us ?

In light of what has occurred in the countries in the southern part of Latin America and Peru, the conclusion is that impunity and its subsequent legalization have triumphed. The triumph of impunity is most obvious in regard to punishment. Those guilty of atrocious crimes in our countries have gone scot-free. The assassins are free men. The rule of law and democracy has been perverted, yet it appears the people can do nothing, as the majority directly or indirectly accepts this perversion. What could be more shameful for a people than to move from de facto impunity to impunity enshrined in law? It is as though evil and injustice had been established as new standards of social life. Thus, the triumph of legalized impunity is tantamount to officially institutionalizing perversion itself, flying defiantly in the face of the people and the world.

However, while one cannot but recognize that impunity and its subsequent legalization have triumphed among us, we must not only express our firm intention to fight it but also ask ourselves about its deep-seated causes. Then, we may find that the phenomenon in question, albeit born in these past 30 years, is actually linked to structural and historical problems in our countries. In a sense, the fight against impunity has become part of the utopian project to build fraternity within each of our societies.[43]

Something extraordinary occurred in Peru when the President of the Republic promulgated the laws providing for impunity, two months after being re-elected by an overwhelming majority (62%) for a second term 1995-2000. For an even greater majority, 87%, expressed its disagreement with the amnesty granted members of the military belonging to the National Intelligence Service sentenced for assassinating 9 university students and a professor – "La Cantuta" case – and released two days after the law was published.[44] Major institutions spoke out against this legislation, in particular the Peruvian Roman Catholic Bishops' Conference and the National Protestant Council (CONEP).

The coalition of Peruvian human rights organizations, the Coordinating Unit, has a gigantic, difficult job in fighting the legalization of impunity. In addition to the overwhelming tasks of defending human rights, the battle must now be waged on another new front, with any number of implications.

From a legal standpoint, the first battle was lost when the Supreme Court of Justice ruled in favour of implementing the laws on impunity. However, depending on the domestic political situation and should the judges have a change of heart, this field of legal action might be re-opened in due course. Furthermore, there will be a new forum for action when the Constitutional Court becomes operational. It is due to be elected by Congress, which has been delaying its appointment since 1993, when the new Constitution was approved.

On a parliamentary level, the overwhelming *oficialista* majority (1995-2000) stands in the way of new legislation in keeping with international law and justice.

A goal set by the Coordinating Unit, which will entail a massive effort, is the holding of a national referendum: for this it is necessary to gather 1,200,000 signatures. Only a serious commitment by a large number of institutions will make a national referendum possible as it is beyond the scope of the Coordinating Unit.

On an international level, in addition to action before the Inter-American Human Rights Commission, the Coordinating Unit has made representations to the various United Nations human rights bodies. An encouraging response was obtained from various rapporteurs of the Human Rights Commission, who sent a letter to the Peruvian Minister for Foreign Affairs stating that "the laws approved by the Peruvian parliament and promulgated by its government foster impunity (...) They contravene the spirit of human rights instruments".[45] This letter was supported by the Human Rights Sub-Commission at its 47th session.[46]

## By way of conclusion

1. The fight against de facto impunity and its legalization is part of the deep, inalienable aspiration for justice that has ever moved human beings to fight oppression. Unfortunately, in Latin America "impunity is one of the central elements at this moment in history";[47] it distorts society as a whole but "particularly affects the poorest sectors".

Therefore, the fight against impunity is part and parcel of a genuine programme to overcome violence.[48] Fighting impunity means rejecting the violence implicit in any form of injustice and building fraternity based on a culture of life and peace, with a non-violent approach. These are the principles that guide the human rights movement and the Peruvian Coordinating Unit[49] in particular.

2. National reconciliation after periods of violence becomes a national political objective. In the case of Peru and many other countries, the governing elites seek to distort the meaning of the words reconciliation and forgiveness, replacing their real sense with one that better suits them. In other words, reconciliation becomes based on the denial of truth, injustice for many and impunity and power for a privileged few. Forgiveness involves only the generous act of the wronged and not repentance and compensation on the part of the wrong-doer. By appropriating the words reconciliation and forgiveness to their own ends, these elites can then accuse "the imprudent justice-seekers"[50] of petty self-interests and attacking peace and democracy.

3. It is essential to reject this debasement of words like reconciliation and forgiveness, and not just for linguistic reasons. The history of former Yugoslavia proves to what extremes the thesis of "burying the past" can lead and the disastrous future it lays in store

for the people. It is not possible for human beings or for peoples to ignore, "to bury their past", as memory is the very foundation of their identity. Thus, experience in various parts of the world "shows us that individual and social reconciliation is impossible to achieve without fundamental respect for a process that includes the notions of truth, justice, recognition of guilt; then, and only then, can there be forgiveness".[51]

## NOTES

1.  Zacarias Cenoce Huayhua's lament when he discovered the body of his wife, who had disappeared a few days earlier from Ayacucho and been executed extra-judicially. The corpses of 18 Quechua peasants – men, women and young children – were also found . "One of the men present cried out in anguish when he saw the body of his wife" states the report of an International Ecumenical Delegation to Peru from 14 to 24 October 1990, pp. 1 and 18. World Council of Churches, Geneva 1991.

2.  The term impunity, according to Louis Joinet, Special Rapporteur on impunity, comprises two facets : a) in terms of meaning, it covers "all the measures and practices whereby, on the one hand, states fail in their obligation to investigate, try and sentence those responsible for violations of human rights and, on the other hand, impede the enjoyment by victims and their families of the right to know the truth and have their rights restored"; b) in terms of scope, the word impunity is used here solely in reference to "violations of a serious and massive nature or constituting a systematic practice", excluding "cases of impunity following reprehensible conduct which is non-premeditated." Cf. United Nations document E/CN.4/Sub.2/1995/18 of June 28, 1995, paras. 4 and 5.

3.  This was how President Sanguinetti justified the laws on impunity enacted in Uruguay with respect to abuses by the preceding military regime. Quoted by Luc Huyse, "Justice after Transition: On the Choices Successor Elites Make in Dealing with the Past", Law and Social Inquiry, Vol. 20, No. 1, 1995. The University of Chicago Press, p. 63, note 48 (subsequently referred to as "Huyse: Justice after Transition").

4.  Cf. Alejandro Artucio, "Impunity and international law", in "No to impunity, Yes to justice", International Commission of Jurists, Geneva, 1993, p. 193.

5.  205. Cf. DIAL, No. D 2038, Lyon, December 1995.

6.  Nelson Manrique, a Peruvian historian, writes in this respect: "This is an uncomfortable subject that generally triggers a series of anxieties when raised here in the country; it is therefore very difficult to discuss it openly"; "perhaps one of the most important discoveries of the social sciences during this period and one of the fundamental tasks facing us in the future is to work to dismantle the mechanisms of racism". In *500 años despues ? el fin de la historia?* Escuela para el desarrollo, Lima, 1992, p. 209.

7.  Cf. Portocarrero, Gonzalo, "Social discrimination and racism in Peru today", ibid, p. 193.

8.  Cf. 1994 Annual Report on Human Rights, Lima, January, 1995, by the Peruvian National Human Rights Coordinating Unit. The Coordinating Unit received the Letelier-Monfit prize (Washington 1990) and an award from the French Government (Paris 1993); it comprises over 40 Peruvian human rights organizations (NGOs and Vicariates of Solidarity) and constitutes a unique experience in Latin America. It now carries considerable weight in Peruvian society and politics.

9. "Shining Path" is a Marxist-Maoist inspired organization that split away from the Peruvian Communist Party in the '60s.

10. Tupac Amaru Revolutionary Movement (MRTA), an organization born of a kind of Latin American Marxism. It began armed activities around 1984.

11. According to the Peruvian review *IDEELE* of the Legal Defense Institute, No.71-72, Lima, December 1994, p. 33 : "...2,526 (10%) belonged to the police force, 11,153 (44.3%) were civilians and 11,503 (45.3%) were presumed subversives"; as the information is generally gathered from the national press through official statements by the Peruvian state, the question of "presumed subversives" is not clear; no one can check the figures given nor the real circumstances of death.

12. Cf. Reports E/CN.4/1993/46, E/CN.4/1994/7, E/CN.4/1994/7/Add.2 and E/CN.4/1995/61 of the United Nations Human Rights Commission. A clear example of this institutionalization can be seen in the case of Lieutenant Telmo Hurtado, guilty of the collective assassination of 62 Quechua peasants – 39 adults and 23 children – in August, 1985. When investigating the case, the Senate was surprised when Lieutenant Hurtado admitted to being the author of the crime, furthermore affirming that it was "proper action (...) that had to be taken to give them (parliamentarians) a better government, stability" and that even 6 year-old children had to die because they had already "been indoctrinated". The War Minister declared to the press that Telmo Hurtado was "fighting for democracy". Following these crimes, the lieutenant was promoted captain. See *Revista Paz, II Época, Año 1*, No. 27, Edita CEAPAZ, Lima, October 1993, pp. 99 and 102. Now, moreover, he is protected by the amnesty granted by the government.

13. Report E/CN.4/1995/36, p.114.

14. See Annual Reports of Amnesty International since 1985 and the annual report of the Peruvian National Human Rights Coordinating Body as of 1990.

15. Report E/CN.4/1995/36, pp.97 to 99.

16. The Working Group was set up in 1980 pursuant to Resolution 1980/20 (XXXVI) adopted by the United Nations Human Rights Commission. Cf. E/CN.4/1994/26, para. 8.

17. Document CAT/C/SR.194/Add.2 dated 22 November 1994, p.2.

18. On the widespread practice of torture in Peru, see the annual reports of the Inter-American Human Rights Commission as of 1991 and, in particular, the 1993-1994 report. The reports of the Special Rapporteur on Torture (Human Rights Commission, United Nations, in particular document E/CN.4/1994/31 dated 6 January 1994). The letters sent by the Peruvian National Human Rights Coordinating Unit to the Committee against Torture (United Nations) on November 4, 1994 and May 18, 1995, requesting the application of art. 20 of the relevant Convention (confidential investigatory procedure for systematic torture). "Amnesty International's concerns about torture and ill-treatment", Amnesty International, London, 1994. "Students assassinated or reported missing", Dossier Pérou, ACAT, Paris 1994.

19. According to figures supplied by the state body in charge of prisons in Peru (INPE), there were 716 persons imprisoned for terrorism in 1988; in 1990, 1,109 and in 1993, 2,867 (of whom 81% were in prison without trial). There are no official figures since that date. The former director of INPE, Mr. Miguel Gonzales del Rio, gave a recent assessment of 5,000 detainees. Cf. *IDEELE* review of the Legal Defense Institute, No.81, November 1995, pp. 19 and 23.

20. Human Rights Watch/America reported that in April 1993 it had received forty-four letters from individuals charged with terrorism in Picsi prison, Lambayeque province, more than half of which contained serious allegations of torture. Each of the 77 detainees interviewed by the Coordinating Unit during its visit to Picsi in September 1994 reported having been tortured during the first days following their arrest. Human Rights Watch/Americas, "Peru, the two faces of justice", Vol. 7, No.9, July 1995, Washington, p. 15.

21. Cf. Report by the International Ecumenical Delegation to Peru, 14-24 October 1990". World Council of Churches, Geneva 1995, p. 15.

22. The representative of the United Nations Secretary-General for internally displaced persons, Mr. Francis M. Deng, visited Peru from August 17 to 22, 1995, and for many Peruvians, it proved "surprising to hear Mr. Deng say the government showed concern and the political will to deal with the problem of displaced persons"; Mr. Deng also took the time to inaugurate no less than a new prison in the company of the President of the Republic, as the Peruvian review *IDEELE,* of the Legal Defense Institute, ironically reported in No.79, September 1995, p. 63 and 64.

23. Cf. "Protection and Assistance for Internally Displaced Persons in Peru" by the International Migration Commission, Lima, 1995.

24. See Annual Reports by the Peruvian National Human Rights Coordinating Unit from 1990 to 1994.

25. Of all those assassinated in cold-blood by the Shining Path, 20% were members of the armed forces or police and 80% were civilians.

26. The role of the armed forces is visible in other countries in the region. Thus, in Latin America, the "caracazo" is sadly famous: a popular uprising in Caracas (Venezuela, 1989) to protest against structural adjustment measures which ended in the death of over 400 people killed by the "forces of law and order". Cf. *Le Monde Diplomatique,* July 1995. In Brazil, armed forces patrol the city of Rio de Janeiro to uphold public order in the face of deliquency, and in Bolivia they help control the activities of coca-growing peasants. Cf. *Semanario Noticias Aliadas,* No.18 (May 18) and 42 (November 16), Lima, 1995.

27. Cf. Jurgen Schuldt, "On the viability of the Fujimori model". *Quehacer,* No.95, DESCO review, Lima, 1995, p. 31.

28. The August 18, 1995, issue of the official bulletin of the Peruvian State underscores the declarations of the President of the Republic, who states that his government had demonstrated in practice that to achieve economic development "it was first necessary to overcome terrorism", thanks, of course, to the Armed Forces.

29. United Nations document CCPR/C/79/Add. dated 5 May 1993, para. 7: "The Committee expresses once again its deep concern on the implications for the Covenant of the Expiry Law. In this regard, the Committee emphasizes the obligation of States parties under article 2 (3) of the Covenant, to ensure that all persons whose rights and freedoms have been violated shall have an effective remedy as provided through recourse to competent judicial, administrative, legislative or other authority. The Committee notes with deep concern that the adoption of the Law effectively excludes in a number of cases the possibility of investigation into past human rights abuses and thereby prevents the State party from discharging its responsibility to provide effective remedies to the victims of those abuses. The Committee is particularly concerned that the adoption of the Law has impeded follow-up on its views on communications. Additionally, the Committee is particularly concerned that, in adopting the Law, the State party has contributed to an atmosphere of impunity which may undermine the democratic order and give rise to further grave human rights violations. This is especially distressing given the serious nature of the human rights abuses in question."

30. Cf. United Nations document CCPR/C/79/Add. 46 dated 7 April 1995 : "The Committee notes that the compromises made by the State Party with respect to its recent authoritarian past, especially the Law on Due Obedience and the Law of *Punto Final* and the presidential pardon of top military personnel, are inconsistent with the requirements of the Covenant" (para. 3); the Committee reiterates its concern that Act 23.521 (Law of Due Obedience) and Act 23.492 (Law of *Punto Final*) deny effective remedy to victims of human rights violations during the period of authoritarian rule, in violation of articles 2, paragraphs 2 and 3, and 9, paragraph

5, of the Covenant. The Committee is concerned that amnesties and pardons have impeded investigations into allegations of crimes committed by the armed forces and agents of national security services and have been applied even in cases where there exists significant evidence of such gross human rights violations as unlawful disappearances and detention of persons, including children. The Committee expresses concern that pardons and general amnesties may promote an atmosphere of impunity for perpetrators of human rights violations belonging to the security forces. The Committee voices its position that respect for human rights may be weakened by impunity for perpetrators of human rights violations" (paragraph 10).

31. Cf. Robert K. Goldman, "Amnesty laws and international law : a specific case". In "No to impunity, Yes to justice" International Commission of Jurists, Geneva 1993, p.218.

32. Advisory opinion OC-14/94 of 9 December 1994 : International responsibility for the enactment and implementation of laws violating the Convention (art. 1 and 2 of the American Human Rights Convention).

33. In this respect, Luc Huyse considers that in democratic transitions, the issue of recognition and punishment become key matters that have to be resolved. Huyse: *Justice after Transition*, p.52.

34. Theo Van Boven wrote: "The world has recently witnessed the fall of several oppressive regimes, the authors of flagrant violations of human rights and fundamental freedoms. (...) In similar situations, a certain number of complex questions have been highlighted, like when to punish or pardon, what are the responsibilities of the government that takes over from oppressive regimes vis-à-vis the victims". "Rights to restitution, compensation and rehabilitation" in "No to impunity, Yes to justice", op. cit. p. 315. Theo Van Boven is the United Nations Special Rapporteur on the right to restitution, compensation and rehabilitation of victims.

35. Cf. "The Amnesty Law and the Barrios Altos Case" in "Peru, the two faces of justice". Human Rights Watch/Americas, July 1995, Vol. 7, No.9, p.43.

36. Cf. Amnesty International, Urgent Action 146/95, 23 June 1995. Mrs. Ana Cecilia Magallanes, the Public Prosecutor who filed the complaint with the Judge, was also threatened.

37. The Public Prosecutor of the Nation, Mrs. Blanca Nélida Colan, declared to the national press that Judge Saquicuray was guilty of the offence of "prevarication". Cf. *IDEELE* Review No; 77, Lima, July 1995, p.4. The same source adds that a few days later, Congress approved a special law to ensure the Public Prosecutor of the Nation remained in her job: her presence was necessary to attain the goals of the laws on impunity.

38. By way of explanation of this abuse of power, the *IDEELE* Review states : "What is happening reflects decisions taken by a powerful lobby comprising civilians and military, headed by Fujimori, brought together by shared secret information (for example, on how La Cantuta crime was decided) and an authoritarian political project in addition to a great deal to hide" (Loc.cit., p.5). Another prestigious Peruvian review shares the same opinion: one hypothesis is "that engineer Fujimori, as supreme head of the armed forces and therefore ultimately responsible for their acts, knew of the intelligence activities that led to the La Cantuta and Barrios Altos killings". *Quehacer,* No. 95, Lima, May-June 1995.

39. The Court ruling upholds a given doctrinal stance and states: "as clearly noted (...), the power to amnesty granted by Congress includes offences and misdemeanors of all kinds as the Constitution does not establish any limitation in such respect; consequently, it is contrary to the law to maintain that amnesty can only be granted for political and not common offences." Cf. File 424-95, ruling dated 14 July 1995, handed down by the Eleventh Penal Court of the Lima Supreme Court

of Justice, comprising Mssrs. Castillo Davila and Hurtado Herrera (the third magistrate, Mrs. Luisa Napa Lévano, cast a different vote, in favour of the Judge's decision).

40. The Court stated that International Treaties: "do not rank as constitutional provisions", "let alone take precedence over a law of the Republic, for were that the case, the Legislative Authority would be limited in the exercise of its legislative powers". Loc.cit.

41. On the primacy of international law in relation to national legislation, see the Vienna Convention on the the the Law of Treaties (1969) – art. 27 : "A party shall not invoke the provisions of its domestic law to justify failure to respect a Treaty" – likewise, the notion of imperative standard (art. 53 on the concept of jus cogens). The Vienna Convention, ratified by Peru, was included in annex by Mrs. Beatriz Ramacciotti de Cubas (p. 631 on), advisor to the current Peruvian govenment, in her book *Derecho Internacional Público, Materiales de Enseñanza de la Facultad de Derecho,* Pontificia Universidad Catolica del Peru, Lima, 1991.

42. In accordance with the principles by which war criminals were tried in Nuremberg (1945), the trial and sentencing of an individual do not depend, in the final instance, on the provisions of domestic law; the primacy of binding supranational standards over domestic legislation is established. Cf. Jacques Verhaegen, "La Protection pénale contre les Excès de Pouvoir et la Résistance légitime à l'Autorité." Université Catholique de Louvain, Brussels, 1969, p. 402f. These principles are subsequently found in other international treaties which provide, therefore, that nothing shall prejudice "the trial and punishment of any person for any act or omission which, at the time when it was committed, was criminal according to the general principles of law recognized by the community of nations." (art. 15, para. 2 of the International Convenant on Civil and Political Rights). Cf. Daniel O'Donnell, "International Protection of Human Rights". Andean Commission of Jurists, Lima 1988, p. 630.

43. The institutionalization of impunity is in no way exclusive to the Latin American and/or "under-developed" countries. In France, for example, there has been only one case – Paul Touvier – in which a French citizen has been sentenced for crimes against humanity; under the Vichy government, no fewer than 75,500 French people of Jewish origin were handed over to Hitler and subsequently perished. Cf. Serge Klarsfeld, "Histoire et Justice" in ... "Que faire de Vichy ?"..., *Esprit,* No. 181, May 1992. Paris, p. 19.

44. This group sentenced for assassination is known in the country as the "Colina Group". Members of this group were involved in another collective assassination, in "Barrios Altos". The national public opinion poll was carried out by a specialized enterprise and the findings published in the national press. Cf. *IDEELE,* loc.cit., p.4. This same "Colina Group", when released, sent death threats to those who opposed the law on impunity; amongst those threatened were three members of the Coordinating Unit's National Board of Directors: the Executive Secretary, Susana Villaran, the Director of *IDEELE,* Ernesto de la Jara, and the Director of APRODEH, Francisco Soberon.

45. Cf. Letter G/SO 214, Geneva, 1 August 1995, signed by the Special Rapporteur on the Independence of Judges and Attorneys, Special Rapporteur on Torture, the Special Rapporteur on Extra-judicial, Summary or Arbitrary Executions and the President of the Working Group on Enforced or Involuntary Disappearance. On the other hand, there has been no public response by Mr. Ayala Lazo, High Commissioner for Human Rights.

46. "The Sub-committee, in support of the initiative taken by the above-mentioned Special Rapporteurs and the President, has decided to postpone consideration of draft resolution E/CN.4/Sub.2/1995/L.47 until its forty-eighth session under item 4 of the agenda". Cf. E/CN.4/1996/2 E/CN.4/Sub.2/1995/51, para. 338.

47. Cf. "Latin American Consultation on Human Rights". World Council of Churches – Latin American Council of Churches. Quito, 24-28 October, 1994. Mimeo, p.3.

48. "Advocacy for justice is integral to building a lasting foundation for peace. All people have the right to resist oppression in their search for justice, peace and a sustainable environment". Cf. "Programme to overcome violence". World Council of Churches. Unit III/CCIA. Geneva 1995, p.95.

49. Its guiding principles are rooted first and foremost in the rejection of violence of any kind. Cf. "National Human Rights Coordinating Unit. Peru", Lima, 1994, p.8.

50. Mario Vargas Llosa, former candidate for the Presidency of the Republic of Peru, added, furthermore, that it is necessary "to bury the past in order to be able to build the future", in an article on impunity in Argentina, "Playing with fire", printed in *Le Monde* on May 18, 1995, p.17. Vargas Llosa never imagined his arguments would be used, one month later, by the President of Peru, Alberto Fujimori, whom he harshly criticized as anti-democratic.

51. Charles Harper, "Exigences oecuméniques pour la réconciliation", in *Université de Paix,* No. 52, September 1995, Belgium, p.15.

# SOME ETHICAL AND PASTORAL REFLECTIONS: TOWARDS A CITIZENS' MOVEMENT AGAINST IMPUNITY

### *Rafael Goto Silva*

## Introduction

In Peru there is a law which affirms impunity as a "basic aspect" of national reconciliation. In order to push the bill through Congress, its drafters defended it passionately, but with little in the way of reasonable ethical arguments. On a number of occasions they sought to justify the law by referring to the Christian roots of forgiveness and reconciliation. For the churches and Christians in particular, these theological allusions to the profoundly Christian gospel values of forgiveness and reconciliation in defending this law represent an ideological misuse and distortion of the meaning of these words. The churches have therefore spoken out and stated their own position on this subject, seeing it as an issue of faith and conscience.

The attitude of civil society has also been very encouraging in that, at all its various levels and by different means, it has made its reaction to this law and to the government's decision quite clear. Never in recent years has a government decision been so widely challenged as this law.

In this paper I shall try to present some thoughts on the implications of this law for true reconciliation in our country and the building of a democratic society.

## I. Implementation of the amnesty law

The first question we have to ask ourselves is: What purpose does this law serve?

The fifteen years of internal war in Peru have left very deep wounds in society, affecting all social, political and ethical relations, not least among the families of the some 25,000 people who lost their lives. Various sectors of society, including the churches and Christian groups, had called for genuine pacification of the country to resolve this situation, as a precondition for national reconciliation, leading to justice for the victims and punishment of those responsible for the deaths and disappearances.

In different ways this feeling has been general and widespread. On the basis of their commitment to the defence of human rights and their ethical convictions, groups of professional people and intellectuals – including some from evangelical circles – called for the truth to be exposed and exemplary punishment to be meted out to those responsible for the horrible crimes committed during this tragic period in the country's history, since there was every indication that they were being concealed from public opinion and the country.

This outcry was based on the fact that of the 25,000 dead, more than 13,000 were people who had nothing to do with the acts of terrorism. They fell victim either because they were popular leaders, workers, peasants and students caught up in these events by other circumstances; or simply because they were what they were – leaders, students, workers, peasants – in short, *the country's poor.*

However, when the congress and government of Peru – which, in the words of its principal spokesmen and the president himself, was seeking for ways to bring genuine peace to the country – approved and enacted the Amnesty Law no. 26479, known as the "Law on Impunity", any hopes of a move in this direction were immediately quashed. Under this law, people who had been responsible for summary executions, for mass crimes, for massacres of children and old people, involving contempt for human life and the most elementary rights of the victims, were allowed to go free and unpunished.

This law showed up the true character of the Peruvian government and the ideological and strategic concepts underlying the anti-terrorist struggle. But it also showed the deep wound this war has inflicted on the sensitivity of individuals and their attitudes to the ethical consequences of their obligations to society and to others. It is a government which some have described as civilian-military, which ultimately subordinates politics to military decisions and action, and ethics, human dignity and life to strategic effectiveness. The underlying message conveyed by these government actions is "*better a dead Shining Path member or subversive than a live one*", so the state quite simply pardons anyone who eliminates subversives.

In earlier years, the government had facilitated the release of Shining Path members facing criminal charges or prison sentences if they confessed and repented. It has sought to justify the law on impunity by this same strategic device, making clear that in its view good justifies evil. The end justifies the means. In the arguments put forward to justify this law it was stated that *in this law the country had a useful instrument for national reconciliation.* Despite his evangelical church connections, Congressman Gilberto Siura, who supported the bill in congress, actually even appealed to Christian ethical convictions in calling for forgiveness for the guilty as an expression of genuine Christian feelings and commitment.

On the contrary, this law has caused a deep break in the relation of ethics to politics in Peru, legalizing a situation which had gradually come to be accepted practice, namely, impunity. On many occasions the advocates of this law drew lines of demarcation between ethics and the political act that had taken place, differentiating between them and situating the implications in different domains. One of them maintained that:

> "*It should be remembered that there is a precise, rational, logical objective behind it.   Let me remind you of a Roman political aphorism: salus publica suprema regis, public health is the supreme law.   That being so, if we are to find peace in this country which has been torn apart since 1980, it is surely worth risking an amnesty.*
>
> *I set the crime committed by some individuals against the good of more than 20 million people and I weighed the two things in the balance – and I decided to vote in favour."* [1]

## II. Reconciliation and impunity: ethical implications

In Christian language, reconciliation is both a gift and one of the church's most important tasks.   The central message of the gospel is reconciliation[2] and the church's ministry is aimed at bringing the *world* to be reconciled with God in order that it may have newness of life.   Christ himself is the author and mediator of this gift and ministry in the church, which is fulfilled in its saving dimension when it is accepted in faith, likewise a gift of God.   The gift of *reconciliation* is also a call to the *world* to accept God's forgiveness. Through reconciliation we are called upon to seek the conditions that will enable people to live in peace, that will establish new relations of human solidarity and build a new community based on fellowship.   Jesus Christ has done all that is necessary and sufficient for human reconciliation that affirms community and human unity: "*For he is our peace*; in his flesh he has made both groups into one, he has broken down the dividing wall, that is, the hostility between us" (Eph. 2:14-15).

*The Christian message is reconciliation.* This is a theological and an ethical statement, and in the context of the approval of the Amnesty Law, it is of singular importance that its promulgation should have been defended by an appeal to this Christian dimension of reconciliation; especially because our people professes and identifies itself as Christian in such a case.[3] But we have to ask ourselves about the motives behind this appeal. We can assume that the reference to the gospel message is a strong appeal to the consciousness of being "peacemakers" inherent in the minds of sincere, practising Christians.   This will always be a deep motive for calling for forgiveness and compassion. But does this call have to be accepted simply because it is made in the name of our faith?

Does it not need to be criticized from an ethical and *Christian* standpoint as a possible distortion of the true principles of the faith?

Accepting the gospel concept, we can say that not all reconciliation is either Christian or evangelical. And this applies to what has been legalized in Peru in the form of an amnesty. The message encapsulated in the Christian concept of reconciliation is not forgetting, but *forgiving.* Contrary to what has been done in the Amnesty Law, reconciliation in that sense starts with the acknowledgement of guilt and acceptance of punishment.[4] Ignoring the sin (or crime) that has been committed is foreign to any approach based on the gospel; reconciliation places the offender and the offended in a position to express themselves to one another, the one confessing and the other exercising compassion. It is very clear that reconciliation implies an act of penitence that takes precedence over other acts in worship, even the most spiritual, going towards the other, the one who has suffered the offence.[5] In contrast to this approach, legalized impunity institutionalizes evasiveness, the concealment of the offender and contempt for the suffering of the victim. Thus, the elements of recognition and solidarity have been lost.

Leaving it up to the offended to accept the offenders and forcing them to "forgive" and forget – as the congress and government of Peru have done – is to *alienate* the principles involved, the rights and duties of reconciliation. What has happened in Peru over the past fifteen years is not an accident in the life of the country. In all this, wills were at work, lives and sensibilities were affected. Very little of what happened can be said to have been accidental or uncontrolled, either. There was much hatred, and human community was broken. For that reason alone it was important that the country should reflect collectively on the implications of this tragic and painful process, in order to acknowledge the guilt and the wounds inflicted and make a start on rebuilding community life. Now this opportunity has been lost.

National reconciliation is incompatible with *impunity.* Nor is national reconciliation something which can be resolved by decree-laws passed by the majority in congress. It ultimately belongs in another sphere – that of daily life in community, of respect for and acceptance of one another, in other words, ethics. Impunity leaves all the rights of the person unprotected and cancels the norms of community life and respect for those who are not in favour with the powers-that-be or are on the margins. From the theological standpoint, it is important also to ask ourselves about the preferential place of the rights of the poor and of the victims in the processes of justice and the application of the laws. It is important, too, to return to the question asked by someone deeply concerned about the problem of reconciliation in his own country: "How can you seek to be reconciled with someone who believes he has done nothing wrong?"[6] The Christian paradigm of reconciliation is the cross, as the expiation for guilt.

### III. Justice as the ethical basis of reconciliation

Another aspect which we need to consider is the relationship of justice to reconciliation. This topic has to be present in any ethical discussion on peace and the well-being of citizens.

*Justice is the basis for the exercise of human rights and harmonious community life.* In this respect, it is the fundamental responsibility and duty of the state to guarantee the conditions that will ensure that relations among its members are governed by justice. From this point of view, there always has to be a legal framework for human rights to ensure they are enjoyed by all individuals and members of society. However, the legal framework which is supposed to guarantee these rights does not always correspond to the situation. At least three conditions need to be fulfilled if human rights are to be realised: a) an organized *de jure* state must exist in the society; b) there must be a pre-established legal framework for the exercise of human rights; c) those claiming their human rights must be given specific legal guarantees that these will be respected.[7] In the absence of these conditions the mechanisms for the respect of human rights are not only not guaranteed, but they are nullified, leaving individuals, especially those who are weakest, exposed to the powers-that-be, and revealing the authoritarian nature of power.

From the standpoint of the gospel, a peaceful society is one *based on justice*. The effect of righteousness will be peace, as the prophet Isaiah tells us.[8] Since this is essential for conditions of justice to be established to safeguard the law, reconciliation in this sense is only one part of a whole. In the Bible there are sufficient theological and ethical grounds for asking society to change the objective, social, political and economic conditions to ensure that all persons, regardless of their origins and their functions or status, are able to live their lives in harmony with others and with their environment. The enjoyment of rights – *all rights*, both individual and collective – is what makes a society and a state not only a legal reality, but *just*.

Consequently, it is inconsistent to appeal to the genuine desire for *reconciliation* but to use it to justify and forget crime, without restoring the rights of the victims. This reveals profound ethical deficit of those who legislate and govern, and highlights the flagrant lack of morality among the governing class. In this context, it is supremely important to seek the prophetic roots of the refusal to accept the present situations in God's own cry against the injustice of the oppressors.[9] In Peru, this cry was heard by Judge Antonia Saquicuray, who defended the fundamental principles of the right to life and the rights of the person, courageously condemning the Amnesty Law as unconstitutional and as a violation of the law and of justice.

It has been noted that the *de jure* state is basic to human rights. This calls for some clarification. In the debate on the amnesty law we also heard some lucid arguments on this from the government benches, which would have offered grounds enough for taking the political and ethical implications of this precondition into account.[10] The rule of law is insufficient if the laws produced under it do not protect the most elementary rights of the poor, the weak, the humble of the country. The option for the right of the poor is the measure of the morality of a nation and of a government. Míguez Bonino says:

> *"A good government....is one which sees its primary responsibility as being the rights of the defenceless who have no means of defending their rights. A good government is measured by the situation in which the weakest of its citizens live. The rights of the poor and the defenceless are the measure of a country's morality."*[11]

The amnesty applied by the government of Peru to those responsible for indiscriminate killings, the rape of defenceless women and girls, and extorsion and abuse against innocent citizens is a *sign* of the injustice and immorality prevailing in the state and among those who govern. It is in itself an expression of the moral illegitimacy of the government which is charged with ensuring unrestricted respect for human rights.

One Christian intensely caught up in Peru's tragedy, and deeply distressed by it, was Fr. Gustavo Gutiérrez, who spoke out prophetically about the situation. In his response to the government's decision, Gutiérrez stated: "We need pacification, but above all we need peace. And we know there is no true peace if it is not built on truth and justice. To set out towards obtaining it is to begin to lose the overwhelming sense of shame that threatens to paralyse us."[12] In relation to this *shame* "we are obliged to seek reconciliation, but on a basis of justice".[13]

*Truth*, like justice, is a basic ethical principle for reconciliation.[14] Untruth distorts the law.[15] The amnesty aims at forgetting, concealing crime, even though the crimes imputed are classed as crimes under common law, acts perpetrated outside the normal run of military duties and action. Article 1 of Law 26479 blatantly justifies and legalizes crime. And it leaves us with no possibility of knowing and finding out more about the events which have brought grief to so many families in Peru.

It does not even censure those who attacked the lives and security of citizens.

Credibility is essential for consistent social and juridical relations and democratic life. The lack of credibility tarnishes any effort at reconciliation and justice. The amnesty law has left a large number of human rights violations in the country uninvestigated, even though by their scale and impact, these have left deep scars in society.[16] Impunity is a consecration of untruth, of concealment, of half-tones, marking the will to survive and struggle against others. In the last analysis this affects not only the individual's relations with the state, but also the events of everyday life. This is quite clearly contrary to the gospel principle that freedom comes from truth.

## IV. Action against impunity by civil society and the churches

Despite all of this, we can still affirm our hope of a return to dignity, basically because of what can be done in Peru through civil society.

In the midst of social and ethical disintegration, we can be confident that society still has moral reserves to draw on to defend its integrity. There is a broad measure of agreement among the communications media, professional bodies, human rights organizations and others, in roundly rejecting this law. The formation of a citizens' movement against impunity and for justice and truth is an ethical expression of civil society demanding justice. This effort to mobilize society in a moral-ethical movement against impunity, involves different social sectors of citizens, so that the struggle against impunity has become an issue on the country's public agenda.

The churches have been working in various domains and in different ways for genuine reconciliation and pacification in the country, and have pastorally addressed citizens' feelings of repudiation of impunity. Both the Roman Catholic Church and the Protestant churches belonging to the National Protestant Council of Peru have issued appropriate pastoral statements condemning this law as unviable.

The bishops belonging to the Permanent Council of Peruvian Roman Catholic Bishops have expressed their concern at "*the grave consequences some provisions of this law could have for social peace and reconciliation, to which the whole of Peru should be committed.*" The Permanent Council also states that "*true reconciliation presupposes that someone who has committed a crime admits it, repents for having done so and tries to make amends for the harm done.*" In their communique released on the day after the law was enacted, the bishops also say that national reconciliation must be based on truth and that it demands justice (Jn 8:32; Lev.19:15). "*If the possibility of uncovering the truth and doing justice is closed, the wounds will not heal, and true reconciliation will not be achieved."* They conclude by pointing out that *"Both sanctions and the reduction of sentences or an amnesty must be inspired by ethical criteria, respect for human rights and the requirements of the common good of society."*

The National Protestant Council of Peru (CONEP), which groups together the country's main large Protestant denominations, has also spoken in similar terms, expressing its *"deep sorrow and indignation at the content of the law and the way in which it was approved. We express our concern at the fact that people who perpetrated crimes against the life and dignity of other human beings are being left unpunished, and above all, at the implications this will have for the consolidation of democracy and the process of pacification."* CONEP concludes its statement by affirming *"the urgent need to seek national reconciliation starting from a genuine expression of the will of the citizens and based on justice and truth, so that the innocent victims of the violence may be cared for and healed..."*

These two statements and the actions which followed in the months thereafter, were a valuable contribution to reflection and to the quest for ways and means of solidarity in building a democratic community in the country. They clearly stated the Christian meaning of reconciliation and forgiveness, both of which are central to the church's mission and the gospel ministry.

## Conclusions

In conclusion, the amnesty law perverts justice by endorsing impunity and authoritarianism. It jeopardizes not only ethics, but the whole stability and credibility of the democratic system in the country. Laws like the one approved on 14 June 1995 in Peru put into question the viability of democracy to guarantee the protection of human rights and repair the harm done to citizens.

Where democracy and the rule of law are weak, crime, whatever its origin, form or content, tends not to be punished, the moral legitimacy of the nation, of society is customarily undermined by practices like bribery, concealment, fraud. The citizens are at the mercy of the strongest who wield power.

National reconciliation, on the other hand, is a task and a process which involves rehabilitating those who suffered the brunt of the violence in the country; but it will also require creating conditions to guarantee the life and rights of the poorest and most vulnerable sectors of the population. According to the gospel, peace is a process involving values such as truth, justice, mercy, forgiveness and equality before the law.[17]

## NOTES

1. The words of Francisco Tudela of the group Renovación, explaining his stance in favour of the amnesty. Tudela is now Foreign Minister in the present government, appointed in July 1995.
2. Romans 5:10-11; 1 Corinthians 5:18-20
3. "...Impunity disguised as reconciliation...". Gustavo Gutiérrez, in "Verguenza", an article published on 18 June 1995 in the newspaper *La República*.
4. Matthew, 5:23-24. It is clear from this text that anyone who claims to worship God has a duty first of all to put things right with those he has offended. This of necessity means admitting guilt.
5. In Christian worship, the confession of sin precedes the eucharist, the Lord's Supper. The essential symbol of the act of reconciliation. Forgiveness implies a change of heart on the part of the sinner, *metanoia:* conversion.
6. Quoted by Robert J. Schreiter, C.PP.S, in *Reconciliation, Mission and Ministry in a Changing Social Order.* p.5
7. Karel Vasak, "Los derechos humanos como realidad legal", in *Ensayos sobre Derechos Humanos*, vol. 1, Andean Commission of Jurists, Lima, 1990, p. 27.
8. Isaiah 32:17
9. See Amos 5:7-15. God's cry can well be expressed in the tears of the families of the 9 university students and 1 teacher, killed and burned in 1992, when the amnesty was passed in favour of their assassins, the paramilitary group Codina. On the implications of this law, see the article by José Burneo in this publication.
10. Dr César Fernández Arce, former member of the Supreme Court, now a member of congress for the government party, noted that: "... very often human beings live separate from the law and plunged into arbitrariness where their will is the criterion that imposes order. And this is bad, because we should all be subject to a legal order which is binding on all equally. Nobody can be above it, because when that happens there is no justice and that legal order falls apart. The fundamental principle if that legal order is to function, is the principle of the equality and dignity of all persons." Taken from the Review *IDEELE*, no. 77, July 1995, p.8.
11. José Míguez Bonino, "*Los derechos humanos de quienes?*", in *Evangelio y Derechos Humanos*, Serie G, no. 6, DOCET-CELADEC, 1978
12. Gustavo Gutiérrez, op. cit.
13. Fernández Arce, op. cit.
14. Isa. 42:3
15. Proverbs 12:17; Isaiah 59:14
16. Amongst other cases, the massacre at Pucayacu (1985), the disappearance of the journalist Jaime Ayala (1985), the murder of prisoners (1986), the assassination of the journalist Hugo Bustíos (1988), the massacre of Barrios Altos (1991), the Cantuta case (1992), the disappearance of the peasants of Valle del Santa (1992), and many more.
17. Revista Paz, II Epoca, Year 3, no. 32-33, Lima, 1995.

# URUGUAY

Reacting strongly in the early 1970s to guerrilla actions by the National Liberation Movement (Tupamaro), the Uruguayan security apparatus and Army heavily repressed all democratic activity and by 1973 had assumed power. The story of the next seven years is one of a police state using classic methods of detention and torture against real and suspected opponents. It is told by the authors of this study, who also describe how a 1989 amnesty law has impeded return to democracy.

# THE CONSEQUENCES OF IMPUNITY FOR URUGUAYAN SOCIETY: A BIBLICAL-THEOLOGICAL APPROACH

## Introduction

*A group theological reflection*

What have we learned from the ending of dictatorship and from the last ten years of democracy? What are the implications of impunity for Uruguayan society? Is it possible to share our experiences with others who did not live through the process in Uruguay? How can we go beyond the merely anecdotal and draw lessons that can be shared with sisters and brothers from other countries, continents and cultures? What theological construction can we put on the consequences of impunity for Uruguayan society? Does the Bible offer us any clues in that regard?

These and other questions have been the main concern of our working group which, in response to an invitation from the World Council of Churches, has been reflecting in recent months on the topic "The Consequences of Impunity for Uruguayan Society".

The working group comprised five persons, four men and one woman, drawn from three Christian confessions (two Roman Catholics, two Methodists and a Waldensian). All have a formal theological education, experience in working in different Christian congregations, in ecumenical service and in human rights organisations. All have long-standing links with the WCC.

We have adopted a biblical-theological approach in an endeavour to analyse and draw the lessons from our somewhat diffuse thought processes of recent years. After an initial round of discussion, each group member chose one or two themes that seemed especially important and by which s/he felt personally motivated, with a view to working on it in greater depth from a biblical, theological and pastoral perspective. The papers that follow are the outcome of this process. All are characterized by their synoptic approach.

Guillermo Kerber compares the covenant between the children of Israel and Yahweh with the one made in Uruguayan society in the form of the Law on the Expiration of the State's Right to Prosecute (Ley de Caducidad de la Pretensión Punitiva del Estado: cf. Statute of Limitations). Luis Pérez Aguirre reflects on the prerequisites for reconciliation and forgiveness. The church's requirements for reconciliation provide pointers of particular relevance to the subject of impunity. Araceli Ezzatti de Rocchietti deals with the reign of fear in Uruguay since the end of the 1960s. Fear as an instrument of social control, and fear on the part of those wielding power are two of the chapters in her study. Carlos Delmonte examines the meaning of tolerance in contemporary Uruguayan society. Ademar Olivera discusses issues of forgetting and remembering in biblical experience, from a political perspective.

## Historical summary of developments in Uruguay since independence

As these studies are addressed primarily to men and women of other countries and continents, it may be useful to provide a brief description of our country.

Uruguay is a relatively small South American country. It has an area of 178,000 square kilometres and 3 million inhabitants with a population growth of 0.8% per annum. It lies south of Brazil and east of Argentina and is therefore bounded by these two countries and by the Atlantic ocean.

The country achieved national independence in 1825. At the beginning of this century it became a model of democratic stability which was viewed as an example by many countries in the region. The separation of the Roman Catholic Church and the state in the early years of the twentieth century set in motion a process of secularization without comparison in South America.

Uruguay enjoyed sustained economic growth until the 1960s, which saw the onset of crisis in the country's economic model. National wealth was based principally on the export of products derived from the country's immense cattle resources, namely, meat, hides and wool.

But the economic dimension is only one aspect of a crisis that is also political, social, cultural and ethical. Growing discontent within large sectors of the population gave rise to an armed minority movement (National Liberation Movement – the Tupamaros), which emerged together with other revolutionary groups in the mid-1960s. Despite the relatively small number of such groups, the government became more authoritarian and declared a state of internal war, unleashing a merciless campaign of persecution against those considered seditious. This included all opponents of the government, whether they were engaged in guerrilla activity or not. Thus began the dismantling of the trade unions, student organizations and other major social organisations.

In 1973, the constitutionally elected President, a civilian, Juan María Bordaberry, dissolved Parliament and installed a dictatorship that was to last until 1984. During that time, thousands of Uruguayans were imprisoned and routinely tortured for political crimes. Some 100 persons disappeared in Uruguay or in Argentina and several thousand fled into exile abroad.

A new Constitution drawn up by the military regime in 1980 was rejected in a popular referendum. That signalled the start of a process of restoration of democracy, in which a major role was played by the mobilization of social forces, international pressure and the discrediting of the armed forces.

After the return of democracy in 1985, a general and unconditional amnesty was granted to all political detainees still being held in Uruguayan prisons.

Very soon, however, the "Law on the Expiration of the State's Right to Prosecute" – also called the impunity law by its opponents – was approved by the Uruguayan Parliament (Law No. 15848 of 22 December 1986). The Law expressly renounced the investigation and trial of culprits in the excesses that may have been committed by the army. After the enactment of the Law, a group of relatives of victims of the dictatorship, politicians, artists and intellectuals constituted the Pro-Referendum Committee for the purpose of calling a referendum on the repeal of the Law. A massive campaign was launched to collect signatures for the holding of the referendum, which was held on 16 April 1989. It failed by a 12% margin (yes-votes were cast on a yellow ballot slip, called the "yellow vote", and garnered 47% of the total over those against it ,"green vote", with 35%).

The role played by the churches varied during the years of military rule. On the one hand, hundreds of Christians from different confessions suffered prison, torture, disappearance and exile for their social and political activism. On the other, the church hierarchies did not oppose the dictatorship outright, though communities, congregations and parishes started organizing themselves and raising awareness, furthering the restoration of democracy.

The following studies offer some thoughts on the manifold implications of the retention of the impunity law for Uruguayan society.

# THE COVENANT:
## ITS STRUCTURE AND CONDITIONS

### *Guillermo Kerber*

## Introduction

The hypothesis we examine is that a new social contract, or covenant, is being enacted in Uruguay with the passing and ratification of the Law on the expiration of the State's right to prosecute.[1] This covenant has a number of characteristics common to all covenants entered into in human society.

The people of Israel are the biblical people of the covenant. Comparison of the covenant of the law on immunity from prosecution with the covenant of God with the people of Israel raises a series of issues which are not settled, but rather remain latent within Uruguayan society and have not yet been faced.[2]

After consideration of biblical evidence, in which I indicate some aspects of the covenant for the people of Israel, I present some ideas on the place of covenants in participative democracy. I conclude my study with a comparison between the covenant of Israel and the covenant of the law on immunity from prosecution.

## The biblical evidence

The idea of the covenant is a central theme in the Bible. For both Jewish and Christian traditions, the covenant God enters into with God's people is the central element in the revelation which is expressed in many forms in the various books which make up the Old and New Testaments.

The history of the people of Israel is the story of the covenant which God (Yahweh) enters into with this Semitic people. With Jesus a new covenant is inaugurated, sealed by his death and resurrection, through which the New Humanity enters into the final covenant.

The covenant of Sinai/Horeb is a paradigm of God's covenant with the chosen people, and thus deserves detailed examination.

As well as declaring the people's commitment to God, the covenant

---

Translator's note: In this article the author uses the words "pacto" and "alianza", the usual Spanish words for "covenant". They can also mean "pact", "alliance" or "agreement". To enable the author's argument to be followed, the English word "covenant" has mostly been used, even when this may not be the natural rendering into English.

also includes a series of rules for human society (cf. Exod. 20:1-17).

The Hebrew word for covenant is *berith*. Its etymology is a matter of debate.[3] However, the linguistic studies indicate that the original meaning of the word carries the sense of "maximum security". *Berith* can refer both to the relation between a superior and an inferior and an agreement entered into by two equal parties.[4] The first type can be seen, for example, in covenants entered into after military confrontations in which the victors grant a *berith* to the vanquished (cf. Josh. 9; 1 Sam. 11).

The covenant of Sinai follows the pattern of a covenant between a superior (the victor or the sovereign) and an inferior (the vanquished or the subject). According to some scholars,[5] this covenant contains the following elements:

1. Preamble
2. Historical prologue
3. Clauses. Words describing the contents of the covenant
4. Keeping the covenant
5. Witnesses to the covenant
6. Blessings and curses
7. Oath of faithfulness
8. Concluding rite

The preamble highlights the solemnity of the covenant by rehearsing the titles and prerogatives of the sovereign. In the covenant of Sinai, this is expressed in the words "I am the Lord (Yahweh) your God" (Exod. 20:2).

The historical prologue is the narrative relating events immediately prior to the covenant or recalling times long past. In our text, the verse quoted above continues, "I am the Lord your God who brought you out of Egypt, out of the land of slavery." This expresses the kindly disposition of the one granting the covenant, usually the friendship and help shown by the sovereign to his subjects.

The clauses give content to the covenant to be entered into. The sovereign freely lays down the conditions, the norms, which were customarily called "words". We should recall here the importance which "word" (Hebrew: *dabar*) has in the theology of the Old and New Testaments. This is seen particularly in the Book of Deuteronomy, which is a compilation of the various laws of the people of Israel. The "word" is a life commitment, an unambiguous expression of the intention of those entering into the covenant.

Covenants were preserved in written form in the capital cities of the kings who had entered into them.

All covenants have witnesses as guarantors that the covenant will be kept. In the covenant of Sinai it is the people themselves who are witnesses to the covenant which God desires to make with Israel.

The blessings and curses call down (and also bring into effect) benefits upon those who keep the covenant and disasters upon those who break it.

The oath of faithfulness and the concluding rite – which was often violent, taking the form of the dismemberment of an animal, to indicate the fate awaiting offenders – conclude and seal the proclamation of the covenant. Once all its stages are completed, the covenant takes on a dimension transcending history.

### Covenants in participative democracies

Covenants between different social and political agents are an integral part of the practice of participative democracy.[6]

Dictatorships do not enter into covenants. People either obey or resist. The claim of the sole power to assert its total authority brooks no disobedience. At most there can be resistance, critical awareness-building, and hope for change.

In democratic society covenants are not simply permissible but actually build up society. They are essential building blocks, which express the diversity of a society.

A covenant also involves abandoning certain courses of action. To achieve a given objective it is necessary to give up certain options. In every covenant analysis and discernment are required to determine which aspects can be surrendered in the course of negotiations for the sake of the ultimate gain and which are the issues that the group cannot give way on. The latter are commonly called "principles". We often say, "We must stick to our principles." But it all depends on what we reckon to be the contents of our "principles".

### The covenant of the law on immunity from prosecution

Some of the elements mentioned above in connection with the covenant of the people of Israel can be extrapolated to the covenant of the law on immunity from prosecution. Philosophical considerations also provide clues for our examination. When we do this, certain issues arise which deserve our attention. The raising of these issues, often in the form of questions, is an invitation to readers to think their own way into the problem.

 a) *Is this a covenant between equals or a covenant between victors and vanquished?*

The law on the expiration of the state's right to prosecute was put forward as the "political solution" to a clear situation: the refusal by the military to allow an investigation into the crimes against humanity committed during the dictatorship. Such political discourse sought to provide legal cover for crimes which will never be investigated.

The covenant of impunity shows that, despite appearances – the end of the dictatorship and the re-introduction of democratic rule – the military continue to hold power and are thus the victors who draw up the clauses of the covenant. The passing of the law gives a legal framework to the position of the military (and the civilians who were accomplices or collaborators in crimes against humanity) at the end of the dictatorship. The signed covenant guarantees "peaceful co-existence" in Uruguayan society and claims to reintegrate the military class into it.[7] We should, however, recall that some cases which were explicitly excluded from the law on immunity from prosecution – such as that of children who have disappeared – have nonetheless proved impossible to resolve, because of the Executive Power has obstructed the work of the Judiciary.

*b)   What sort of security is expressed in the covenant?*

As mentioned above, by derivation the word *berith* means "maximum security". We should now be asking ourselves what security is achieved by the covenant of impunity? There are several possible answers: the re-introduction of democratic rule, the "return of the military to their barracks", the re-establishment of political parties, and an end to the state of emergency under the dictatorship.

Whicn of these, one or several, were uppermost in the ratifying of the covenant? It is very difficult to decide. Probably a combination of several, and others we have no idea of, operated in the collective consciousness of the people to ratify the law.

It is, however, beyond doubt that the issue of security played a key role in bringing the matter to a conclusion.[8]

*c)   What course of action is being abandoned?*

It is explicitly stated that investigation into the crimes committed by the military during the dictatorship is abandoned. But is not something else being abandoned? Is not the pursuit of justice being abandoned? Can a society abandon the search for justice? What are the consequences of such an act?[9]

With the law on impunity an attempt has been made to throw a cloak of oblivion over crimes committed over a period of years. Is it possible for the families of those detained and disappeared to abandon. their desire to know what has happened to their loved ones?

"Those who forget history are doomed to repeat it" runs the phrase by Santiyana posted at the entrance to the Dachau concentration camp.[10] Can a society refuse to be informed about so significant a phase of its life?

Moreover, some of the victims of repression during the dictatorship, after making repeated claims to the state, have received financial compensation. In this way a material ethic has prevailed, since the sanction of the law on impunity has made the investigation of the crimes committed impossible. Any type of moral redress, which is what really matters, is ruled out.

*d) Who are the parties to the covenant?*

The making of a covenant implies at least two parties. Who are the parties giving the covenant on impunity their seal of approval? One party can be clearly identified as the military, although in this category are also included civilians who occupied positions of responsibility during the dictatorship: the President of the Republic, ministers, members of the Council of State – the body which replaced the Chamber of Representatives and the Senate – and those who collaborated with the regime at various levels. But, who was the second party? Uruguayan society? The Uruguayan people? The politicians? The traditional parties? [11]

*e) The people as witnesses?*

The people of Israel were a party to the covenant and witnesses to it, guarantors of the Sinai covenant. What was the place of the Uruguayan people in this covenant? Formally, the people were represented in Parliament when the law was passed by the necessary majority. Moreover, they were consulted by means of a referendum, the result of which ratified the law.

But the expressed will of the people does not necessarily make the chosen option the right or appropriate one. The people of Israel did not only enter into the covenant of Sinai. They also built and worshipped an idol, the golden calf (Exod. 32). It is possible for human beings to act contrary to God's will, as is evident in the fact of sin and the faithlessness of individuals and of the people as a whole.

## Conclusion

Uruguayan society is today experiencing the effects of having impunity built into its life. The passing of the law on impunity marks a significant break with the country's institutional and democratic history.

The covenant of the law on immunity from prosecution is a covenant of death savagely directed at the most vulnerable members of society. When crimes against humanity remain unpunished by the will of parliamentarians and the people, what will happen with other human rights violations, which are apparently less serious than torture, murder or disappearances? Thus, as impunity infiltrates and penetrates the various levels of society, alongside it other evils become acceptable, such as fraud and corruption at all levels, violence in the home against women and children, ill-treatment of suspects by police, the inhuman conditions in Uruguayan jails, raids and violence against young people, in short: a lack of respect for life.

The infringement of the rights of the most vulnerable groups is the result, on the one hand, of the introduction of neo-liberal economic policies into our country. While the per capita Gross National Product increases and the economy is stabilized, government cuts have left public education, health and social security in a desperate state. On the other hand, presenting terrorism as the new enemy[12] makes it more possible for the police and armed forces to repress by branding any sort of demonstration against the government as "terrorism".

The churches cannot stand aside from this issue. Because, as well as being communities of faith, from the viewpoint of political philosophy they are societies embodying the experience of the people of Israel and of the various Christian communities over thousands of years of history. Their contribution to an ethic for contemporary democracies is thus indispensable. In order to make this contribution, contextualized theological insights are essential to enable a response to the challenges of the present to be made. It is that conviction which has inspired what is written here.

## NOTES

1. As regards the "Law on the expiration of the State's right to prosecute" (cf. Statute of Limitations), see the relevant paragraph in the introduction. The word "covenant" (Spanish: "pacto") has been repeatedly used by politicians. Recently, in July 1994, in a judgment on the forced disappearance of a child during the dictatorship, the Minister of Defence again referred to the Law on immunity from prosecution as "a covenant established in Uruguayan society."

2. The events of 24 August 1994 are a tragic example of this. In a confrontation between police and demonstrators, at least one person died and about one hundred were injured. It should be noted that during the whole period of the dictatorship, no one died in public confrontations with the police or military in the course of mass demonstrations.

3. In these paragraphs, I am following J. Shildenberger in the article on "Alianza" (covenant) in *Diccionario de Teología Bíblica*, Herder, Barcelona, 1967, pp.32-40.

4. Cf., for example, J. Schreiner, in "Los orígenes del pueblo de Dios" (The origins of the people of God) in idem., "Palabra y mensaje del Antiguo testamento" (Word and message in the Old Testament), Herder, Barcelona, 1972, pp.79-81.

5. I am here following the presentation and comments of M.A.López in "Éxodo. Estructura y esquema general de la alianza" (Exodus. The general structure and pattern of the covenant), duplicated, undated.

6. For some of the ideas followed here I am indebted to Paulo Botas, a Brazilian philosopher living in Campinas.

7. In the eyes of the Uruguayan public, however, the military have lost the dignity

and respect they enjoyed as professionals in the period before the dictatorship. This is a value judgment which is very difficult to substantiate.

8.  It was not fortuitous that one of the bulwarks of the military regime was the Doctrine of National Security. Security, with strong mythical overtones, was one of the most important values during the period of the dictatorship. I believe that this value, emphasized out of all proportion, has left its mark on the collective unconscious of the people.

9.  The events of 24 August 1994, referred to above, are not irrelevant to this issue.

10. Paradoxically, this was also one of the catch phrases used by the military dictatorship in reference to the violence by urban guerrillas at the end of the 60s and the beginning of the 70s.

11. The traditional parties are the Colorado Party and the Blanco (National) Party, which have alternately held power during the whole democratic history of the country. With slight variations (the Colorado Party was originally the party of urban areas and the Blanco Party the party of rural areas), they hold a conservative ideology, which in recent years has swung between liberalism and neo-liberalism. Recently, important candidates have taken on social democratic ideas in their speeches.

12. The Minister of the Interior, the President of the Republic and other government representatives repeatedly had recourse to this device in connection with the above-mentioned events of 24 August 1994.

# RECONCILIATION, JUSTICE AND FORGIVENESS

### *Luis Pérez Aguirre*

> *"I am writing so that death*
> *may not have the last word"*
> Odiseo Elytis

The quotation which opens this reflexion helps us to focus the complex theme of reconciliation properly, in terms of the memory a people must retain of the crimes and violations of human rights in order to counteract the evil of impunity and its most pernicious effects.

My purpose here is to show the reasons a people has for forgiving and being reconciled while not forgetting what has happened. This has to do with the imperative need to ensure that what has happened should not be repeated and that what has been learned through immense suffering should benefit not only those who are still struggling to staunch the wounds, but also the new generations who watched appalled the horror of a cruelty it is hard to explain rationally.

When we in the Service for Peace and Justice in Uruguay decided to commit ourselves to the struggle against impunity and for a process of national reconciliation, we were actually making an unbreakable commitment to the people of Uruguay. It is difficult to sum up in a few words what prompted us to do so, because there were many pressing reasons for it. But briefly, I would say that our motive was the same as that of our sisters and brothers in Brazil, Argentina and Chile and it has been summed up in a statement which has become part of the heritage of our suffering peoples, who have been the victims of the so-called "Doctrine of National Security" and of "state terrorism". As Julio César Strassera, the Public Prosecutor, said at the end of the memorable trial in Buenos Aires on Wednesday 18 September 1985 at 15.25 hrs: *"We have the responsibility to establish a peace based not on forgetting but on remembering; not on violence but on justice. This is our opportunity: perhaps it will be the last. Your Honours, in closing this interrogation let me explicitly abandon any claims to originality. I use a quotation which is not my own, because it belongs to the people ...Your Honours, – NEVER AGAIN!"*

Argentinians, Brazilians, Uruguayans, Paraguayans and Chileans have all had to struggle to lay the foundations for a national reconciliation which will also guarantee the re-establishment of justice.

Besides the victims' elementary call for justice there was the obligation to do everything possible to prevent any recurrence of what happened to us in the period of the dictatorships. And the first thing was to know the full magnitude of the disaster we had suffered.

In this connection it is important to draw attention in particular to the situation of those who disappeared, because it is an extreme instance of "otherness": a society which accepts the principle of impunity deprives these people of all human qualities. They are denied their humanity! In effect they are deprived of the last link they had with society. They are denied even the right of being at a particular place at a particular time. And the members of their families live in a twilight world of doubts and imaginings. They are left in a state of constant torture and cruelty. In extreme cases (without speaking of the children who disappeared) they could not even bury their dead who have never been found. As a result they have not been able to mourn and work through their grief. There is no doubt in my mind that this open wound, this darkness in the soul surrounding those who disappeared, casts its shadow beyond the immediate families concerned and begins to affect the whole of society.

Because of all this we must make it our duty to dismantle the mechanism of impunity, and to look for effective ways of forgiveness and reconciliation. If we cannot show that impunity no longer has any place in our countries because we have got at the truth of what happened and justice has been done, our peoples will be committing political "hara-kiri"; they will be moving along a precipice towards social suicide. This is so simply because to leave the theory of impunity intact is to tell the Mengeles and the Barbies that they can walk freely in our streets, that no-one can expose them or bring them to justice, confirming them in their belief that terrorist activities in the context of the state go unpunished; that it will never be possible to know what happened or who exactly was responsible, and that ultimately justice cannot touch them and can always be flouted.

To close wounds and be reconciled does not mean to forget. Forgetting is a sign of weakness and fear of the future. The crimes took place; they are unpunished and they are in the collective memory of the nation. Our history is made by what the people keep in their memory. They will have to keep in mind the undeniable fact of these crimes – for they are now part of our history. But let us not also add impunity to that history; let us rather add the capacity for forgiveness and reconciliation. The purpose of investigating these crimes is to help create the conditions for this to happen. It would be sad if we were to keep for ever in our collective memory the fatal fact that we showed ourselves to be a fainthearted people who allowed ourselves to be cowed by miserable threats from a few of the military, forcing us to forget the criminals and leave them unpunished. It would be intolerable to live always with our own shame and lost dignity. Peace, which is always the fruit of justice restored, would then be an unattainable, nostalgic illusion.

And here the collective memory has a key role to play – not in judging, because the judges and the provisions of the constitution are there for that – but in protecting the present which has its roots in the immediate past. We have to be able to call on memory in order to establish our own identity, to recognize what is ours and discover it in that amalgam of griefs and hopes, because without memory – as Monsignor Cristian Precht has put it so well in the introduction to *Chile: Memoria Prohibida* ("Chile's Forbidden Memory") – "we do not know who we are. Without memory we wander aimlessly, not knowing where to go. Without memory there is no identity."

The collective memory helps us look at history and learn from it, trying to shed light and use words where darkness and silence have reigned. It shows us an undeniable guiding principle – namely that history in general records only the deeds and words of those who were able somehow or other to hold onto life and give it meaning and express it. But there are huge numbers of men, women and children who have been deprived of dignity through crime or terror or lies, and as a result have been silenced. The victims who were able to complain and whose voices were heard had a better fate. Memory has to show the other side of words and light. Those whose fate it has been to survive must assume responsibility for that silence, and for the shadow cast by our history, if they are not to be its accomplices.

The truth is that when an act denies the essential humanity of human beings, any solution which seeks to absolve it of guilt in the name of some ethic or other contradicts morality itself. To forget past crimes would be to commit a new crime against the human race. Every crime is an outrage against a person as a human being, not against "X or Y" ... as a communist, a left-winger or an ideological opponent. And what in fact happened is that all morality was abolished in order to control society for certain specific purposes. How are we to explain to the coming generations that any given policy may call for the disappearance of children?

Forgiving is not forgetting, which in this context would be a sign of weakness or of fear of the future. Neither is it indifference, which fundamentally implies a flight from reality through lack of convictions;

nor is it *naïveté* that is prepared to believe everything and open to the manipulation of conscience.

Many people think that forgiveness and reconciliation are almost human weaknesses, symptoms of timidity and cowardliness. There is a kind of nefarious "machismo" which can think only in terms of revenge or violence if it is not to feel humiliated or inferior. But this attitude is based on a misconception and a confusion. Forgiveness is confused with weakness and courage with vengeance or being unable to forgive; whereas in fact the truth is very different. It takes great courage to be able to forgive and act accordingly ... Contrary to what is generally thought, forgiveness is a difficult, risky act – it is the attitude of strong and noble people. It can only happen when someone has really injured another in his or her being or rights. Therefore it is not a matter of forgetting or indifference, far less *naïveté.*

Forgiveness always is and must be a magnificent gesture. People who are able to forgive consider that someone who has injured them is less of a person than the one who has suffered injury – their action aims at breaking that magic circle of evil – that "armour-plating" with which evildoers surround themselves. Those who truly forgive are trying to break that fateful circle in which all human communication founders ... Forgiving involves risks because it relies solely on the hope that the good-will offered may open up a corner in the wrongdoer's heart where there will be room for a logic other than the logic of evil. Those who forgive do not want to be imprisoned in the evil emanating from their opponent. Slander is not put right by slander, nor one false accusation by another, nor deceit by deceit nor aggression by aggression. The aim is to create a new relationship – forgiveness invites us not to allow evil to have the last word.

It is also important to state that *one cannot forgive in the abstract.* One cannot forgive through someone else, a third party, because forgiving the wrongdoer would then be tantamount to cruelty towards the victim! Only those who have actually been tortured or robbed can forgive the wrongdoer in question. Only those who have been the object of hatred and the victims of the wrongdoer's destructive intention can truly demonstrate the powerlessness and stupidity of hatred. Only those who hope that what they do will create a new history of amicable relations between them and the person who hates them can truly forgive that person.

It is also important to explain to Christians that indignation and anger at an unjust enemy are not sins but genuine feelings of the individual who welcomes the Word of God. In the Bible we see on countless occasions that indignation and wrath are not only morally "tolerated" but express a prophetic moral censure. In the Old Testament we find many passages in which these feelings and in some instances even shame are expressed as censure directed at the enemy, for instance this from Psalm 58 [Vulgate Psalm 57]:

> *Do you indeed decree what is right, you gods*
> *Do you judge people fairly?*
> *No, in your hearts you devise wrongs;*
> *your hands deal out violence on earth.*
> *...*
> *O God, break the teeth in their mouths;*
> *tear out the fangs of the young lions, O LORD!*
> *Let them vanish like water that runs away;*
> *like grass let them be trodden down and wither.*
> *Let them be like the snail that dissolves into slime;*
> *like the untimely birth that never sees the sun.*
> *sooner than your pots can feel the heat of thorns,*
> *whether green or ablaze, may he sweep them away.*
> *The righteous will rejoice when they see vengeance done; they*
> *will bathe their feet in the blood of the wicked.*
> *People will say, "Surely there is a reward for the righteous;*
> *surely there is a God who judges on earth."*

And this is by no means an isolated Old Testament text. I could quote many others like it – and in the New Testament too – in which God himself feels anger and indignation (Romans 2:5-8). I believe that when one interprets Christianity as something mild and romantic, proclaiming impossible harmonies and unities which do not exist – and are therefore false – one lapses, albeit involuntarily, into complicity with unjust oppressors and aggressors. In the Psalm I have quoted, as in so many other extremely stern biblical passages, one of the major themes of the Word of God stands out clearly: justice.

The mighty – those with the power, those who have weapons with which to kill, those who attack and rob the poor – seem to swing the balance of history in their favour; but a God arises who confronts them and does justice and will disarm them and shift the balance away from them. Because, says God, justice there will be. And that God will avenge the "little ones". Reconciliation can never be contrary to the justice for which the poor in their anger and indignation cry out with a heart-rending clamour.

I draw a compelling conclusion from the biblical message: we cannot love the oppressors and the oppressed in the same way. We love the oppressed by standing alongside them in their struggle to free themselves from their oppression and their poverty. We love the oppressors by condemning them, combating their injustice so that they may be brought to abandon their attitude and be capable of restoring dignity to the sisters or brothers who have been robbed of it, so that they will be able to live as children of God. The oppressors must depart from their violence to be able to overcome the alienation it entails and live in fellowship. Christian love is always a demanding, creative love with a specific focus, able to be discriminating in each instance – which is neither naive nor easy. It is never a recipe for an impossible harmony or a fictitious "unity"; it is a daily challenge (Cf. James 5, 1-6).

In the gospel Jesus never tells us we have no enemies. What he does tell us is that we must love... Moreover, the fact is that if we want to live out that gospel in a society where there is conflict, with social, economic and political inequalities we shall have enemies. Loving one's enemies does not mean we are blind to them. The truth is that as Christians we are called to love those we think of as opponents in social and political terms; but this does not mean we have to stop thinking of them as opponents or treating them as such. Frequently if not always, loving one's enemies in practice means condemning and rejecting them. Here love takes the form of a struggle. We love our enemies so that they will stop being unjust and alienating their brothers and sisters – and not by naïvely believing that to love them means putting ourselves in their hands. By struggling against them in their injustice we shall be showing them ways for them to change, because loving one's enemies must always be aimed at freeing them from the situation of oppressors and aggressors, into which they have put themselves. It must be clear that Christian love never excludes conflict. It takes account of conflict. The Christian challenge is this: to love in the midst of conflict – to love effectively.

Jesus loved his enemies. But that very fact clearly implies that he had them – and many of them. He never concealed that hostility, but expressed it – in the strongest terms – and fully accepted the conflict. His enemies ended by torturing him and murdering him in the cruellest way. The leading priests, the groups who controlled doctrine and theological learning – the scribes and Pharisees – and the imperial forces of Rome in Palestine were Jesus' enemies. He courageously condemned all oppressive situations which kept the people in subjection, and he never yielded to the standpoints of those who were in power. Thus he loved them in a wholly genuine and realistic way, lashing them with his word, questioning their modes of behaviour and the rules they had unjustly imposed on the people.

Division, whether within a Christian community or the national and international community, is generally a symptom of sin. But if we look at division from another angle it can be a sign of the presence of Jesus and the demands of his gospel. He himself put it this way:

> *Do not think that I have come to bring peace to the earth; I have*
> *not come to bring peace, but a sword.*
> *For I have come to set a man against his father,*
> *and a daughter against her mother, and a daughter-in-law*
> *against her mother-in-law ...*
>
> (Matthew 10:34-35)

We already had an advance signal of this conflict which characterizes the good news of Jesus (good because it proclaims equality among brothers and sisters, but with conflicts in the midst of divisions) in the description of the meeting of old Simeon with Mary and her baby. Simeon tells Jesus' mother:

> *[Behold] this child is destined for the falling and the rising of many*
> *[in Israel], and to be a sign that will be opposed so that the inner*
> *thoughts of many will be revealed – and a sword will pierce your*
> *own soul too.*
>
> (Luke 2:34-35)

In a society which has been dominated by injustices, the demands of the gospel – creating relations of equality between individuals, putting the last on the same footing as the first, sharing everything etc. – are bound to cause huge conflicts which will not be resolved by forgiveness that is artificial and merely skin-deep. Any attitude of true forgiveness must accept that conflict and start from the reality of the conflict itself. Hence, as I have said, forgiveness is a challenge, and a demanding one.

Jesus told us that we should forgive "seventy times seven" – that is, "always" (because there he was using a typically oriental set of numbers). Forgiveness among sisters and brothers is an essential element in the gospel – an element which involves risks.

**Between individuals**

When we forgive another person, we risk being mistaken, hoping that if we place our trust in that someone, this gesture will suffice to shake that person's conscience and heart and make him or her change, so that there will be a reconciliation, a fresh encounter. Jesus did this on many occasions – with Matthew, with Zacchaeus, with Nicodemus ... He entered into a new relation with them, forgetting all prejudices, forgiving what had been done in the past in order to achieve a future that would be different.

Forgiveness is therefore a positive attitude, profoundly optimistic in regard to human beings. Those who forgive believe in human beings and believe they really are capable of changing and that evil does not have the last word. Christian forgiveness is really excessive (though never naïve) *trust* which causes a person to put himself or herself in the hands of the other person, confident in the hope that the latter will change. And that hope is nourished by the whole community. Forgiveness is an unqualified gesture aimed at overcoming situations where there is a total breakdown in relations. This was Jesus' practice with individuals.

## In society

But one cannot talk of forgiveness or reconciliation in the same categories when we move from the sphere of relations between individuals or between a community of brothers or sisters, to that of a society in conflict. In this instance, forgiveness and reconciliation have to be analysed amongst other things on the basis of political categories, which are not so simple and uncomplicated. There are no recipes or magic formulae. The fate and life of many people are at stake here. And the risks have to be measured from different standpoints. The vicious circle of acts of revenge, retaliation and vengeance will always have to be overcome – but never at the cost of drawing enemies, injustice and all, into the community by dispensing with a thorough, serious analysis of their intentions. The shepherd never puts the wolf into the sheepfold.

In this dynamic of not simplifying the issues, the churches have never granted forgiveness and reconciliation with the [Christian] community to anyone who had sinned unless the person fulfilled certain elementary requirements – certain conditions set forth in all the catechisms, viz.

1.  to examine one's conscience
2.  to repent of the evil committed
3.  to resolve firmly not to do it again
4.  to confess guilt before the community and God
5.  to carry out an act of penance to make amends for the injury done

Pope John Paul II put this very clearly in his encyclical "On the Mercy of God" (no. 14) when he said:

*It is obvious that such a generous requirement of* forgiveness does not cancel out *the objective* requirements of justice. *Properly understood, justice constitutes, so to speak, the goal of forgiveness.*

> *In no passage of the Gospel message does forgiveness, or mercy as its source, mean indulgence towards evil, towards scandals, towards injury or insult. In any case reparation for evil and scandal, compensation for injury, and satisfaction for insult are conditions for forgiveness.*

We may conclude by saying that every human being, by the very fact of living in a specific country and at a specific time, with its contradictions, struggles, progress and regressions, is involved in a dialectic of conflict. God's message and God's plan appear in the midst of that conflict. Therefore it never is nor can be a "neutral" or impartial message. It is an altogether one-sided message, biased on the side of the oppressed, of those who suffer injustice, and in their favour – a message starkly opposed to the oppressors. God is biased in favour of the little ones and the "sinners" – Jesus tells us – as opposed to the rich and the oppressors who think they are "good" and pure because their social status allowed them to conform to legal regulations. We live our lives in that historical situation of conflict and it is the context where we have to put our Christian commitment into practice by trying to effect reconciliation as the basis for fraternal relations. God does not speak in the clouds, he speaks in the conflicts of history. He speaks in circumstances. And it is up to us to make our history with its conflicts and contradictions into a salvation-history in which forgiveness and reconciliation reside.

# UNDER THE REIGN OF FEAR:
# FEAR AS AN INSTRUMENT OF SOCIAL CONTROL

### *Araceli E. de Rocchietti*

> *"Alas for those who devise wickedness*
> *and evil deeds on their beds!*
> *When the morning dawns they perform it,*
> *because it is in their power". (Micah 2:1)*

Some years ago while visiting a former Nazi concentration camp in Germany, we saw that it was an old farm near to several towns. The group's question was obvious: how was it that the people living in the surroundings saw neither the trains arriving nor the smoke? The guide answered tersely: "Crimes of such monstrosity need many accomplices... most often the whole nation."

That answer reminded me of the growing involvement of the Uruguayan people throughout the 10-year dictatorship. Of course, it started years before, with signs that we overlooked: the law on education, persecution of trade unions, strike breakers, black lists, the closing of newspapers and of other communications media. There were also more subtle devices such as rumours, denunciation, dismissal of militants or even dissidents, for preposterous reasons. Above all deep-seated and generalized distrust had seriously undermined human relations within the family, neighbourhood, place of work and centres of learning.

The role of the people in facilitating this process of dictatorship was by commission – all those who collaborated; or by omission – those who were passive, or chose not to see. Uruguay is a very small country with a highly homogenous population and no large isolated groups. It was very difficult not to see, hear or have some idea of what was happening. That is why I maintain that this process was a collective act that changed all of us Uruguayans and which had a social cost of which we have still not fathomed the full implications even now, after ten years of democracy.

Uruguayan society has not traditionally been silenced. On the contrary, it has a long tradition of political and trade union activity, open discussion of national issues, and even of thriving artistic and popular forms of expression.

The years prior to the dictatorship were particularly rich in that regard. Nevertheless, by systematic and organized campaigns both nationally and internationally, the civilian and military authorities succeeded in: limiting the vocabulary by banning certain words, burning books, closing down meeting places or centres of learning. *Fear cuts communications*: repression became more and more brutal, ranging from simple identity checks to people being beaten up in the street, disappearance, torture and death. Fear was an effective instrument created by state terrorism, causing collective paralysis and gradually snuffing out any actions that challenged or confronted the authorities. It is important to note, however, that new and sophisticated ways were devised for circumventing the repression and gradually building up resistance to it. Though not always successful, that resistance paved the way, at home and abroad and with the invaluable help of international solidarity, for the emergence of a democracy which may be lacking and deceptive in many respects, but which should not be underestimated.

## Fear on the part of the powerful

> *"Ah, you who make iniquitous decrees, who write oppressive statutes, to turn aside the needy from justice and to rob the poor of my people of their right, that widows may be your spoil and that you may make the orphans your prey!"* (Isaiah 10:1-2)

> *"The next day, that is, after the day of Preparation, the chief priests and the Pharisees gathered before Pilate and said, "Sir, we remember what that imposter said while he was still alive, 'After three days I will rise again, 'Therefore command the tomb to be made secure until the third day; otherwise his disciples may go and steal him away, and tell the people, 'He has been raised from the dead,' and the last deception would be worse than the first."*

> *Pilate said to them "You have a guard of soldiers; go, make it as secure as you can." So they went with the guard and made the tomb secure by sealing the stone"* (Matthew 27:62-66).

When the Armed Forces finally had to open the prisons in 1984, having taken upon themselves the task of safeguarding *National Security*, there was irrefutable evidence of the enormity of what had taken place during the years of such harsh repression. The rights of thousands of citizens had been violated, destroying their interpersonal ties, their health and their lives by attempting to eradicate their ideas and those of generations to come. Those of us who waited along the road leading to the prison, located in the middle of the town of "Libertad" (freedom), will never forget that long line of freed prisoners, weak, their hair close-cropped, poorly dressed, as they embraced their family and friends, clinging to them for support as they dragged along their meagre possessions. Nor can we forget how the people lined the 60-km road to Montevideo, greeting them with banners and large bonfires. Up to that time we believed that the democratic process was well under way... but historical processes are neither simple nor lineal. Fear on the part of those responsible for so much abuse prompted them to start creating networks for their own safety.

The passage from Matthew 27: 62-66 sheds much light on this situation. The high priests and Pharisees appeared before Pilate after the crucifixion of Jesus, *worried* about the business of the Resurrection and above all the possible impact on the people of a Christ dead and risen again. Why approach the civil authority with a theological matter, why fear a dead man? Why should the army be needed for reassurance? Why should there be doubt as to the effectiveness of their own premeditated act of killing Jesus? Why is there now talk of a mistake? Could it be that these men learned in the law of God began to realize that they had chosen the wrong path? That the Word of Life cannot be silenced by force? That Jesus killed and risen was already in the kingdom of the just? The History of Salvation tells us that stones and weapons were not enough to seal the tomb.

This fear also existed in Uruguay. When a surprised population slowly began to react, they expressed anger, pain, and they demanded justice. The counter-reaction was not long in coming. Once again, though now in a democratic setting, the instruments of disinformation and intimidation were set in motion to justify and as far as possible to remove the evidence of the aggression to which we were subjected for 10 years by our compatriots as if we were mortal enemies.

This process of "removal" of the evidence once again necessitated the creation of a vocabulary to whitewash events: social unrest in quest of rights was called *war;* militants became *subversive and unpatriotic;* repression became *protection of respectable citizens;* torture, *over-zealousness in the discharge of duty* ... unconstitutionality, *state of emergency.* Fear was now gripping those who had wielded power with more arrogance than authority, more weakness than strength.

## False amnesty, or pardon without repentance

The outcome of the referendum approving amnesty for the armed forces was a harsh blow for many people, a sharp slap in the face of those most harmed by the dictatorship, those who were and are still seeking their loved ones who disappeared. But as already stated, these processes are not lineal. Our democracy is still tarnished by dictatorship and a sector of society is still mesmerized by the increasingly "stylish" look being given to domination through all the talk of restoring social peace and fostering economic development.

I would venture to think that there has not been sufficient time to evaluate the deeper ramifications of the dictatorship for Uruguayans and Uruguayan society. In this process of deterioration in the quality of life, which is worldwide, the ideals of social justice which we find in the Gospel as the announcement of the Kingdom of God should be upheld by the "least" and by the remnant, who are prepared to risk all. As a matter of the greatest urgency, we should launch a process of clarification on the part of all groups in society:

*"For our struggle is not against enemies of blood and flesh, but against the rulers, against the authorities, against the cosmic powers of this present darkness, against the spiritual forces of evil in the heavenly places"* (Ephesians 6:12).

There can be no process of national reconciliation without the repentance that means humbling ourselves before God in prayer and fasting, open to guidance by his grace along the hard road back from the darkness of fear and hopelessness towards the light of reparation, forgiveness, reconciliation and of peace that needs no weapons to safeguard it.

The church's call to humility and repentance is difficult to put across when the arrogant words of power and authoritarianism are resounding so strongly in society. Only the profound conviction born of faith in a God who is the Lord of history, and in the reconciling power of grace, can make the Christian message announcing true salvation through Christ's death and resurrection truly prophetic.

*"For when we were still weak, at the right time Christ died for the ungodly. Indeed, rarely will anyone die for a righteous person – though perhaps for a good person someone might actually dare to die. But God proves his love for us in that while we still were sinners Christ died for us. Much more surely then, now that we have been justified by his blood, will we be saved through him from the wrath of God. For if while we were enemies, we were reconciled to God through the death of his Son, much more surely, having been reconciled, will we be saved by his life. But more than that, we even boast in God though our Lord Jesus Christ, through whom we have now received reconciliation"* (Romans 5:6-11).

# TOLERANCE IN A PROCESS OF RECONCILIATION

### *Carlos Delmonte*

According to the dictionary, "tolerance" is "respect and consideration for the opinions or practices of others, even though we may find them repugnant". The term "to tolerate" means "to endure with patience".

I believe that Uruguayan society has displayed tolerance, not just in a generic sense of excusing the unlawful, but also as a quest for justice based on respect for the human person of those who, for their opinions and practices "are repugnant to them".

Following the enactment of the "Law on the Expiration of the State's Right to Prosecute", the groups that were pressing for investigation into the events that had caused human rights violations under the military regime showed a great sense of tolerance. No vengefulness could be detected on the part of those victims who continued their endeavours for justice to be done.

When the Law was about to be put to a referendum, we called a meeting in the Waldensian community to discuss the matter. We had a very large turn-out. People representing all shades of opinion attended the meeting, where everyone said what they were thinking, and spoke frankly for or against the law. People who had previously militated in opposing groups discussed that sensitive topic with dignity and mutual respect. Everyone was convinced that an atmosphere of understanding could be created and the meeting demonstrated that it was possible to discuss matters in a spirit of fellowship. We were all convinced that we could still discuss this topic in a spirit of mutual tolerance.

We had another example of that spirit one Sunday when there were two baptisms. One couple who had participated actively in the guerrilla movement and had suffered years of imprisonment and torture as a result came to have their daughter baptized. Despite all the hardship, they were now rebuilding their lives, happy at the birth of their daughter, whom they wished to have baptized in our community. The other couple in-cluded a young soldier who then had the rank of lieutenant, the son of an army colonel.

In the meeting preparatory to the act of baptism I felt it was only right to explain to the couples just whom they were going to meet at the Sunday service. The couple who had militated in the urban guerrilla asked if that posed a problem for the church. I told them that it posed none, that on the contrary the service would be highly meaningful for the whole congregation. The husband then said: "Oh, I thought you believed that God thinks like us." The couple with the lieutenant who had participated in bloody clashes with the guerrilla said that for them it was precisely in the church that reconciliation should take place. The two little girls were baptized at the same service and we all saw the ceremony as a concrete example of tolerance.

Nevertheless, we must admit that tolerance is like a delicate plant that must be nurtured. The violent clashes of 24 August 1994 sparked off by the extradition to Spain of three Basque citizens for trial on suspicion of belonging to terrorist organizations showed us just how fragile our tolerance can be. Tolerance has its price. It calls for active and unwavering commitment, for patience, and above all it means striving towards an understanding among everyone, something that cannot be taken for granted. Tolerance will thrive only if it is rooted in love.

Here we see the churches' responsibility very clearly. In their reflection and in their preaching of the Word of God, the churches must go forward together. It would seem that in present-day Uruguayan society love is also called tolerance. We must decide whether we are all prepared to pay the price of that tolerance, whether we are ready to make common cause against all obstacles that might prevent that tolerance becoming a concrete reality.

# FORGETTING AND REMEMBERING

### *Ademar Olivera*

## Defining terms...

"Forgetting" and "remembering" are closely interrelated terms, like two branches of the same tree. We cannot speak of the one without taking the other into account.

"Forgetting" means not remembering, or no longer thinking about a past event ("amnesia": loss or impairment of memory).

Forgetting may be a necessity, an imperative that acts as a defence mechanism, for someone who has had a traumatic experience, for instance. Hence a "sleep cure" as a form of therapy or relief.

But the opposite is just as true: remembering, bringing to the surface of the conscious something that is buried in the subconscious, could well be the only cure for a patient suffering as a result of a shock in the past.

Forgetting and remembering are mental attitudes that reveal very deep-seated sentiments, and sometimes independently of the will of the individual. Forgetting or remembering may relate to an individual or a collective experience.

Memory plays a highly important role in the life of a person or a people, as it enables us to know who we are and to affirm our identity.

## A Bible reading...

Forgetting and remembering both have deeply religious significance. The Bible affirms that God has a good memory, that he does not forget his children, his promise of life and liberation:

> *"But Zion said, 'The Lord has forsaken me. My Lord has forgotten me'. Can a woman forget her nursing child, or show no compassion for the child of her womb? Even these may forget, yet I will not forget you"* (Isa. 49:14-15).

On different occasions, God's people are given the command not to forget, to keep alive the memory of God's liberating action in history, of the Covenant, of his great love:

> *Then the Lord said to Moses, "Write this as a reminder in a book..."* (Exodus 17:14).

*"So be careful not to forget the covenant that the Lord your God made with you..."* (Deut. 4:23).
*"...and when you have eaten your fill, take care that you do not forget the Lord, who brought you out of the land of Egypt, out of the house of slavery..."* (Deut. 6:11-12)
*"Bless the Lord, O my soul, and do not forget all his benefits..."* (Ps. 103:2).

The oral transmission of the Word of God, his commandments and his teachings not only entailed the use of memory, but also enabled God's people to know history and to preserve their identity and the relationship between each generation and its forebears:

*"But take care and watch your-selves closely, so as neither to forget the things that your eyes have seen nor let them slip from your mind all the days of your life; make them known to your children and to your children's children – ..."* (Deut. 4:9).
*"When your children ask you in time to come: What is the meaning of the decrees and statutes and the ordinances that the Lord our God has commanded you? then you shall say to your children, 'We were Pharaoh's slaves in Egypt..'"* (Deut. 6:20-21).

The theologian Gustavo Gutiérrez stresses the importance of memory in the practice and in the transmission of faith:

*"The Bible is historical. Memory is important. The memory of past historical deeds is evoked in order draw attention to Yahweh's liberating action in the present... 'It was not with our fathers that Yahweh made this covenant, but with us, with us who are here, all living today' (Deut: 5,3). The covenant has been struck today. It is not a fact confined to the past. Biblical faith, however, besides being memory, is freedom:* **openness to the future**. *Recalling the liberating deed of Yahweh is not the nostalgia of bygone days. All the great love contains the memory of the first moment. In strong moments it is the fount of gladness, in difficult moments it is the reaffirmation of hope. In either case the gaze is to the fore. The future is the task. Memory thus has the function of conditioning a creative liberty..."* [1]

In the New Testament, Jesus told his disciples that in celebrating the sacrament of Holy Communion they should: *"...Do this in remembrance of me."* (Luke 22:19). In the Eucharist, faith endows memory with singular importance.

The author of the Letter to the Hebrews underlines the importance of the recollection of the struggle, of resistance to injustice and of solidarity with those who suffer as genuine witnesses of faith:

> *"But recall those earlier days when, after you had been enlightened, you endured a hard struggle with sufferings, sometimes being publicly exposed to abuse and persecution, and sometimes being partners with those so treated. For you had compassion for those who were in prison..."* (Hebrews 10:32-34).

On some occasions, if the past threatens to destroy hope for the future, forgetting takes on creative and fertile meaning:

> *"...No-one who puts a hand to the plough and looks back is fit for the kingdom of God"* (Luke 9:62).
> *"Not that I have already obtained this or have already reached the goal; but I press on to make it my own, because Christ Jesus has made me his own. Beloved, I do not consider that I have made it my own; but this one thing I do: forgetting what lies behind and straining forward to what lies ahead, I press on towards the goal for the prize of the heavenly call of God in Christ Jesus"* (Phil. 3:12-14).

## A political reflection...

It is clear that some political and military circles use those terms in a calculated way designed to paralyse action, in order to prevent possible investigation or trial of those accused of crimes against humanity. There have been numerous recent instances of this in our countries in the Southern Cone, as mirrored in the following expressions:

"No need to keep looking back"; "we must turn over a new leaf"; "we must put a veil over the past"; "full stop"...

When the cynic affirms that "nothing happened here", what he really means is that thanks to the impunity enjoyed by the aggressors, "the same thing could happen all over again".

The history of a people, with its watershed events, is formed not only of accounts and interpretation by professional historians, but also comprises personal testimonies and experiences that come to form part of the collective memory.

The decision to forget traumatic events from the past is only of value if taken based on the truth acknowledged by the protagonists and voluntarily by those affected.

A society such as ours, which underwent a traumatic experience, must confront, accept and analyze that past in order to comprehend how such degrading and perverse events could have occurred. If the truth of what happened is not acknowledged and revealed, the wounds will remain open, damaging the fabric of society.

It is very important to learn from the past so as to avoid any recurrences. That was one of the aims of the series "NUNCA MAS" (publications relating events that took place under military dictatorships in Argentina, Brazil and Uruguay).

During the trial of the Nazi leader Klaus Barbie more than 40 years after the events, Simone Weil, a French writer with first-hand experience of Nazi atrocities, said:

> *"I believe that we must never forget, because forgetting would in a way be accepting that things can happen again. Forgetting implies considering that what happened was of little importance... I believe that we must always examine and know about the past, though in a forward-looking perspective"* (Brecha, 29.05.87).

Edmundo Gómez Mango, in an article published in *Brecha* on 13.04.89 (before the referendum, for the green vote in our country), deals with this subject:

> *"Amnesty (which means forgetting) is as old as politics. Political life must come to terms with the need to forget and to remember. Human societies have always used strategies, customs and policies with regard to forgetting and remembering. To heal, the wounds in the collective civil memory also call for a healing process based on thought and language. The winners do not wish to remember, the victims do not wish to forget. For them, the antonym or the opposite of forgetting is not memory, but injustice. In the life of society there is no duel – the possibility of expressing rage and vengeance – without justice."*

Hebe de Bonafini, the president of the "Mothers of the Plaza de Mayo" in Argentina, said on that same occasion: "If one does not triumph, an explanation must be given of the reason for not forgetting the past, not for the sake of vengeance, but because it is always necessary to know the truth. It is through the memory of the people that it is possible to work towards the future" (Mate Amargo, 20.04.89).

## NOTE

1. Gustavo Gutiérrez: "The Power of the Poor in History", p. 12.

# ARGENTINA

General Martín Balza, the present Army chief of staff, recently admitted that the military and security forces in the "dirty war" of the 1970s had not been justified in using illegal methods against thousands of detainees. Despite seven years of atrocities, and an unprecedented trial of high officers in 1985, two laws were subsequently passed during the tenure of President Raúl Alfonsin (*Punto Final* and *Obediencia Debida*) which exempted the vast majority of officers and agents from trial by court. Today the still unknown whereabouts of many of the disappeared remains a gaping wound in public consciousness and the body politic. Conservative estimates of those civilian victims who are presumed dead during this period come to 20,000. There remains, twenty years later, a profound sense of frustration and injustice among large sectors of the population.

# THE CHURCH: A WITNESS TO THE TRUTH ON THE WAY TO FREEDOM

### Raul Soza

In the history of our continent – and in much of the South of our planet – the decade of the seventies was marked by the quest for liberation. In the economic field, developmentalist proposals were confronted by the "dependence theory".[1] In the socio-political field, peoples' liberation movements went from strength to strength. The prominent role of the "theology of liberation" also showed clearly that the church too was not unaffected by that momentum.

The eighties, for their part, were marked by a profound call for truth. Violations of human rights and the forced disappearances of thousands of Latin American men and women – perpetrated by the military dictatorships – set up in our continent an urgent call for the different situations there to be clarified. The truth was thus seen as a fundamental condition if all the violence that had been experienced was never to be repeated, and if the new democracies were to be able to rely on strong support. And just as, in the seventies, the quest for liberation was not only a Latin American affair, so too in the eighties the demand for truth was also felt in the countries of the East because of the clear need for "transparency" [*glasnost*].

Today we should perhaps ask ourselves whether for the next few years we do not have to make a determined effort fruitfully to inter-link those two demands which seemed to belong to the past. I am convinced that democracy will only become firmly established if it is able to provide a sound basis for both freedom and truth. And freedom will be real freedom, and not merely ideological talk, only in so far as it contains a large measure of truth. For its part, the quest for truth will become most fruitful when it is constantly set in the perspective of freedom.

### Confronting two views of truth

From its beginings the Christian faith was placed between two ways of looking at the truth – the Jewish and the Greek ways.[2] Truth in the Greek sense – [the noun] *al'theia* – means, basically, clarification, bringing into view something which has been concealed. For the Greeks, therefore, the quest for truth implied an exercise in making something transparently clear, i.e. bringing out the meaning as clearly as possible, without distortions or perversions. This line of thought had great influence on the concept of knowledge in the West and particularly on the view held about much of theological knowledge. Defining the truth as "making the meaning  transparent" and as "explication" has been characteristic of theology, with its aim of understanding reality in its deepest form and seeking to free faith from all myth and historical error. Theology grounded in this mode of understanding truth has pursued the intelligibility and relevance of the faith in the midst of circumstances which tend to obscure it and make it irrelevant. Following this line of Greek thinking, knowledge comes to have the character of understanding.

But we must not forget another characteristic of the Greek view of truth: its non-temporal nature. Truth is not something that happens – it is something already there, which is intrinsically beyond time; consequently it is also immutable. That which is true endures, and what is transient conceals the truth. Thus, to *know*, one has to go beyond the transient and withdraw from the dynamic of history. Only in so far as one can free the object to be known from its historical relativity is the truth attainable. True knowledge is "pure", completely objective knowledge. This characteristic of *al'theia*, where to know is to try to arrive at the truth beyond its bondage to the historical moment, has undoubtedly greatly influenced Christian faith and theology. This view of truth and this mode of knowledge have given us  a non-historical and immutable view of God, and reduced faith to a kind of *gnosis* and theology to a mere practice of orthodoxy.

The other, Jewish view of truth has also influenced the faith since its beginnings. The Hebrew word for truth is *emeth*. According to Pannenberg,

> **Emeth** *is not on hand once and for all as a timeless, binding state of affairs. Rather,* **emeth** *must occur again and again. ... Thus, in the Israelitic sense, truth is "reality (which) is regarded as history ... not something that in some way or another lies under or behind things, and is discovered by penetrating into their interior depths; rather, truth is that which will show itself in the future."*[3]

This dual dimension in the Jewish view of truth is interesting. One dimension is *trustworthiness, reliability*. Here truth is that in which one can put one's trust; we arrive at the truth of something not only when it is clear and verified, but also when we can place our faith in it. Truth is that which we experience as an inescapable challenge to commit ourselves to what "now we see in a mirror dimly" (1 Corinthians

13:12) in the certainty that we shall see it "face to face" in the future.

The other dimension of the Jewish view of truth is its contingent, *historical character.* Truth is not something pre-existent – already a complete datum; rather it is something which continues to gestate, is "done" or enacted, and "occurs again and again".

> *All the paths of the Lord are / steadfast love and faithfulness, / for those who keep his / covenant and his decrees.* (Psalm 25:10)
> *But those who do what is true come to the light, so that it may be clearly seen that their deeds have been done in God. (John 3:21)*

As we see from these biblical texts, truth in the Jewish view is never independent of history nor of enacted history. "Truth" is always something that is *done* – that which *becomes* truth. In the Psalmist's words, it is a *path* on which to travel, a way of behaving, a mode of acting.

Perhaps these two views of truth – the Greek and the Jewish – are not mutually exclusive, but complementary, opening up a fuller and deeper panorama for faith and theology. All the following are tensions which neither faith nor theology can disregard: understanding and believing; meaning, explication and transforming commitment; confirmation now and future fulfilment; reason and experience; the mind and the heart. But both faith and theological knowledge have frequently distanced themselves from these tensions, favoring the Greek view. This has had consequences which have not only impoverished theology but have also distorted faith itself. Non-historical orthodoxy, rationalism and spiritualized religion are distortions which have frequently marked the church's life and continue to do so.

## Truth and freedom

The entire Bible indicates that truth is not an abstraction beyond history, but few texts present this to us as clearly and categorically as the prologue to John's Gospel:

> *And the Word became flesh and lived among us, and we have seen his glory, the glory as of a father's only son, full of grace and truth (John 1:14).*

Truth is not only *linked* to history, it has already *become* history in Jesus Christ. In his life, death and resurrection the truth has been concentrated in such a way that it cannot be separated from history without betraying it and reducing it to mere ideology.

### Ecumenical leader urges former Argentinian oppressors to confess[4]

**By Dafne Sabanes Plou**

**Buenos Aires, 18 April** – A prominent religious leader in Argentina has urged members of the military during the country's dictatorship from 1976 to 1983 to end the cover-up on the period by confessing their participation in massive human rights violations, including numerous murders.

"The history of humanity teaches us that it is very difficult for the conscience to escape the blood of our brothers and sisters that cries from the ground itself," said Rodolfo Reinich, president of the Evangelical Church of the River Plate (Lutheran-Reformed) and co-president of the Ecumenical Movement for Human Rights.

"We encourage all those ready to leave aside the ... 'silence agreement', to recognise their participation in reprehensible activities and to declare publicly all that they know."

Reinich was referring to members of the security forces who helped repress political opposition during the Argentinian dictatorship. Only now are members of the security forces beginning to confess their actions.

"The Word of God, along with thousands of years of experience, teach us that truth and justice are indispensable values in the search for deep reconciliation and a lasting peace," Reinich said. "This is why we agree with those who ... affirm that reconciliation in a society can only take place if responsibilities and sins are publicly recognised with total honesty."

Reinich's message, made public just before Easter, follows a public confession by a former navy captain, A. Scilingo, who admitted that he had taken part in the killing of political prisoners who were thrown from navy aircraft into the River Plate, near Buenos Aires.

These murders took place in 1976 and 1977. Scilingo said that many navy officers were forced to take part, and were bound by a "silence agreement" involving all officers in the security forces.

Scilingo said that about 2000 prisoners were thrown from aircraft, though their deaths were never reported. A total of about 30,000 people went missing during the dictatorship.

Other officers have already given evidence to a government commission investigating the fate of missing people. Their testimony has been used in the trial of members of the military juntas that ruled Argentina during the dictatorship.

Recent confessions from former navy officers have included some startling allegations about Roman Catholic military chaplains and about Pio Laghi, Apostolic Nuncio, the Vatican's representative in Argentina during the dictatorship. It has been alleged that Laghi, an Italian who now holds the rank of cardinal, visited concentration camps during the dictatorship and had a friendly relationship with the then navy head, Emilio Massera. The pair often played tennis together.

Massera is believed to have been the main official responsible for the concentration camp located at the Argentinian Navy School. It was the point of departure for aircraft loaded with the prisoners destined to make the terrifying and fatal fall.

The country's Roman Catholic bishops have tried to defend Pio Laghi's position during the dictatorship, saying that the Nuncio did "his best to save lives", and that some prisoners were freed and sent abroad as political exiles thanks to his negotiations with the military.

But these declarations, backed up by a pastoral letter signed by five progressive bishops on Palm Sunday, 9 April, have failed to convince the public of Laghi's innocence during the dictatorship.

A major debate has now begun about failure of the Roman Catholic hierarchy to intervene forcefully to protect human rights when the military juntas were exercising repressive policies and violating human rights.

Other Protestant leaders, including Methodist bishops Federico Pagura and Aldo Etchegoyen, have declared that "the religious [officials] involved ... have to be part of this search for truth so that they may not be considered to have been in complicity with this silence".

According to Reinich, "self-justification that tries to deny or forget the past ... will always be an obstacle to true peace".

Konrad Raiser, general secretary of the World Council of Churches, sent a letter before Easter to Reinich and Bishop Etchegoyen, supporting their pastoral work with the victims of military repression.

Raiser expressed support for their work and with former members of the military and security forces who want to own up to what they have seen or experienced.

"We share your conviction that confession opens the door to pardon and reconciliation," Raiser said.

"We believe, like you, that this will help to heal your moral wounds and those of the entire Argentine people," Raiser wrote. "Be assured of our support and prayers for your pastoral ministry in these challenging days."

If truth has become history in Jesus Christ as never before, seeking the truth means being radically willing to follow Jesus. Faith ceases to be "adhering to a series of correct propositions", and becomes a *discipleship*, deciding to live one's life in the way Jesus has shown. We find the truth when, in the midst of our everyday reality, we accept the call of the one who says "I am the way, and the truth, and the life" [John 14:6].

The Gospel of John goes even further. Truth is not only related to history, but is also linked with freedom in the person of Jesus and in following Jesus.

> *Then Jesus said to the Jews who had believed in him, "If you continue in my word, you are truly my disciples, and you will know the truth, and the truth will make you free". (John 8:31f.)*

The Exodus is a fundamental experience for our faith,[5] an experience of salvation. The People of God are called to freedom. Without any doubt, to have faith in God means to be faithful to that call to seek freedom for ourselves and for others. Thus liberty echoes in the minds and hearts of Christians. The Christian faith is *proved true – verified –* and becomes the truth in the quest for freedom.

In the dynamics of faith freedom is our deepest vocation for life, and truth is the path that leads us to it. For Christians, this path leads through Jesus Christ.

So, then, to probe deeper into this relation between truth and freedom – a relation essential to the Christian faith – it is appropriate to ask ourselves why Jesus Christ is the truth which leads us to freedom.

Jesus himself was a free person. He was free from bondage to the Mosaic Law because, through the Spirit, he did not yield to the casuistic Jewish interpretation of the law, but viewed the Law from the standpoint of love. Jesus was free to break with the taboos and prejudices of his age which marginalized and discriminated in the same way our prejudices do today. He was free from the ambitions for power which were a strong temptation both for him and for his disciples. He was free to experience an intimate, personal relation with God as opposed to that form of piety which made the Temple the essential way to God. Jesus was free to choose his friends and disciples from among the most ordinary "little ones", and not the learned and the important. He experienced the call of freedom so radically that he could give his own life in witness to this call and to God's promise.

Because Jesus experienced freedom so fully, he is the "true way" to freedom, and a deeper, more genuine relation with God.

The freedom he experienced inspires our own hopes to live freely. The freedom which is incarnate in Jesus Christ is the freedom which calls the church to be a people, a community, and not an "institution" or a caste of "priests".

## Truth frees us from lies

Erich Fromm has taught us that "freedom" is comprised of "freedom from" and "freedom for".[6] Without both there is no full or genuine freedom.

What does the truth free us from? It certainly seems too simple and obvious to state, as we do in the sub-heading, that "truth *frees us from* lying". But if we try to go beyond the obvious we shall discover meanings which are very relevant for us today. For reasons of space I shall mention only three of those meanings which are closely interrelated.

Lying is not only an individual act – something which takes place at the level of personal relations. It is also a social act, part of the web of political, economic and social relations in Latin American countries – to mention only what is closest to us. What is more, lying does not happen in isolated acts but has become a methodology of both political and economic power. When lying takes root in society it eventually becomes institutionalized. To give a concrete example, *corruption* has reached great proportions of social lying.

Institutionalized lying becomes even more serious when power legitimizes it. This legitimizing of corruption leads to *unpunished evil – impunity.* Impunity may mean failing to do justice where human rights are being violated, or it can be permitting crimes against creation or letting jobs be cut for thousands of men and women because they are not competitive in the Free Market. Impunity can take various forms in society, but in the last analysis it always involves legitimizing falsehood.

Corruption and impunity do not occur in isolation from each other. They are the two poles of a social dynamic of falsehoods which support and reinforce each other. The combined effect of these two elements is to produce a third element, *disbelief,* which in turn becomes an integral part of lying. In a society where corruption and impunity prevail in the corridors of power, lack of credibility characterizes the image of the ruling class, and distrust takes hold of the people.

It is unnecessary to illustrate this further. The problem becomes even greater when corruption, impunity and unbelief begin to be such normal and everyday affairs that they no longer even shock us.

The consequences of this dynamic of falsehood are a significant part of what is oppressing and enslaving us personally and socially.

Therefore it is necessary and urgent that the call for truth should be taken up much more forcefully than is the case at present. Only if this happens shall we be able to take the first steps on the path towards liberation from institutionalized and legitimized lies.

The church cannot stand apart from this quest for the truth. God has called it to be the chief actor in this quest in the body of society. This task is not incidental or secondary. It is in fact the very essence of mission. As the Apostle Paul wrote to Timothy: "the church of the living God, (is) the pillar and bulwark of the truth" (1 Timothy 3:15)

### The tuth frees us to transform the reality

The freedom to which the gospel leads us, the truth that we find in following Jesus is always a "freedom for", a call to transform the world:

> *I am not asking you to take them out of the world, but I ask you to protect them from the evil one. They do not belong to the world, just as I do not belong to the world. Sanctify them in the truth; your word is truth. As you have sent me into the world, so I have sent them into the world. (John 17:15-18)*

Where does this capacity for transformation have its roots? First of all in the fact that the truth always questions the "reality". It is much more than a neutral explanation of the established order, and still less can it be turned into something which justifies leaving things as they are.

The truth always places "reality" in a crisis by *judging* it. This judgement constitutes the first step towards transforming it. Life lived in the truth cannot remain indifferent in the face of personal or social sin: truth names sin, and condemns it. Truth does not conceal evil, it makes it visible.

We can appreciate that for the Bible the truth frees us to transform reality. Because both in the Old and the New Testament *truth and justice* constantly appear together. Truth becomes *verily* true – it is *verified* – in the exercise of justice. If the truth that has become incarnate in Jesus Christ does not free the Christian from selfcenteredness and fears which prevents a commitment to justice, we are not living the truth – it is "not in us". Truth is always precisely itself, and acquires its historical significance to the extent that it produces acts of justice.

This point is one which has to be stressed in our day. In Latin America where neo-liberal winds have so recently been blowing, we have become accustomed to hear the political and economic authorities singing the praises of freedom. Neo-liberalism has produced talk about freedom which tries to convince us that freedom can be measured in terms of our willingness to "privatize" public companies. We are free when we agree to "deregulate" so that big corporations can cut production costs by using cheaper labour, without any concern about unemployment or the workers' quality of life. The more consumer opportunities, the more freedom – even although most people cannot afford even the basic necessities.

This Free Market freedom is not the freedom the Gospel proclaims. The truth proclaimed and lived by Jesus Christ leads us to a freedom characterized by justice. Jesus appealed to Isaiah's words:

> *The Spirit of the Lord is upon me, / because he has anointed me / to bring good news to the poor./ He has sent me to ... proclaim / release to the captives / and recovery of sight to the blind, / to let the oppressed go free, / to proclaim the year of the Lord's favour. (Luke 4:18 - 19)*

We have been freed to transform reality because Christ did not separate truth and justice.

Truth is a transforming force when joined with *love for one's neighbour.*

Both Peter and Paul make this link between truth and love an essential element of freedom[7]. John in his first letter states it most clearly and forcefully:

> *We know that we have passed from death to life because we love one another. Whoever does not love abides in death. All who hate a brother or sister are murderers, and you know that murderers do not have eternal life abiding in them. We know love by this, that he laid down his life for us –and we ought to lay down our lives for one another. How does God's love abide in anyone who has the world's goods and sees a brother or sister in need and yet refuses help? Little children, let us love, not in word or speech, but in truth and action. (1 John 3: 14 - 18)*

Truth Christians confess is confirmed in love of our neighbour. Faith which is not translated into a love that becomes a historical reality distorts and falsifies the cross of Christ.

The love which true faith demands of us is not just any love, but love which opens itself to the sufferings of the neighbour to the point of sharing the goods we possess.

This truth, lived out as a commitment of love to those who suffer, enables us to achieve freedom and leads us to undertake the exodus from death into life. The absence of love places us in the sphere of falsehood and makes us slaves to material goods. Thus life does not thrive in us and we remain in thrall to death.

The neo-liberalism which prevails today makes it necessary to highlight this challenge to live a life of love sensitive to the sufferings of others. The absolutizing of the Free Market is much more than an economic recipe or formula. It represents a culture, a "way of being" which is both personal and social, characterized by profound indifference. John uses the word "hardening" of the heart [John 12:40]. When indifference captures the "heart" the purpose of life for which we were created – communion with God and our neighbour – is betrayed.

The neo-liberal model will only survive if it succeeds in "hardening our hearts" to the sufferings of those who are paying its prices. Only truth which is historically rooted in love and justice can free us to transform it, our lives and the lives of others.

## Truth calls for consistency

In an age so full of unbelief, the church cannot live as if it still had automatic credibility through its history and institutions. The church must become credible in order that the world might believe (cf. John 17:21).

For its witness to be credible the church must let itself be borne on by the breath of the Spirit of truth. *When the Spirit of truth comes, he will guide you into all the truth.* *(John 17:13a)*

A church which lives by the power of the Spirit of truth is a church willing to commit itself to those who suffer most by condemning lies and sins, calling for more love and more justice, and proclaiming a freedom which is not merely a disguise for oppression and slavery.

A church which lives in the Spirit of truth is a church which has also resolved to live a life of love, justice and freedom *ad intra* – within itself.

Just as there are many instances where the church has remained aloof in face of the violations of human rights, massive poverty, and institutionalized lies in society, so too there are many examples of the lack of love, justice and freedom within it.

Only if the church shows greater determination in ridding itself of this will it be able to proclaim – with the authority of Christ – that we have been created for freedom, and that the path which leads us there travels by way of a truth that becomes a historical reality by living love and justice.

EVANGELICAL METHODIST CHURCH OF ARGENTINA
Buenos Aires, 6 March 1995

Press Statement

The families of disappeared persons, the public at large and political and military authorities have been shaken in different ways by the confession of the former Lieutenant-Commander Adolfo E. Scilingo. His statements confirm the painful truth of what happened to thousands of persons subjected to an unusual form of capital punishment, with neither trial nor judgement, but merely by decision of the military authorities in power from 1976 to 1983. His statement could be another chapter of "Nunca Más" (Never Again) by CONADEP (Argentine National Committee on the Disappeared), and yet another addition to the numerous allegations by human rights organizations of torture, disappearances and killings perpetrated by those who were in charge during this most dismal chapter in our country's history. The former Lieutenant has been expelled from various positions of authority; nevertheless, the Prophet Ezekiel states the following truth in the Bible:

> "But if the wicked turn away from all their sins that they have committed and keep all statutes and do what is lawful and right, they shall surely live..."

We welcome his attitude of repentance, although his revelations have brought distress to many. Will there be other confessions? Are there other men and women still carrying in their heart and mind such profound remorse, and who could display the same courage? They should know that Jesus reminds them today: "... and the truth will make you free."

More than a political-military topic, this issue pertains to faith and ethics, as it has to do with truth and life. The conspiracy of silence surrounding these aberrations is a clear sign of cowardice and choosing that option is a denial of any Christian conscience. Silence is the seed of impunity, the fruit of which is hypocrisy and falsehood.

We believe that the former lieutenant's confession, in addition to affecting the Armed Forces, is the true path to genuine reconciliation. Undoubtedly, all of this also holds implications for the democracy that we are trying to consolidate on the basis of truth, justice and morality. It is also surely bound up with a new conception of military power that would henceforth replace the motivations that led to so much pain and death.

We cannot help thinking of the thousands of relatives who have been deeply distressed by these disclosures. We remember them in our prayers.

This development raises two challenges. First, it challenges the religious authorities concerned and the government to join in the quest for the truth rather than themselves becoming accomplices in silence. Second, it is a call for disclosure of the lists of persons kidnapped and killed, so that the families concerned may learn what became of their loved ones. Failing this, the full truth will still not come to light.

Bishop (E.) Federico J. Pagura     Bishop Aldo M. Etchegoyen

# NOTES

1. The developmentalist ideology explained the poverty of the South and the wealth of the North as different phases in the same process of development: the North had reached the stage of being developed while the South still remained in an earlier stage – "under-development". The solution for this "under-development" was to take the North as the goal and model. The dependence theory revealed that the poverty of the South is not a stage prior to the wealth of the North but the reverse of that wealth. Wealth is there on the one hand because of poverty on the other. There are not any developed and underdeveloped countries but "mother countries" and colonies that are dependent on them. Consequently overcoming poverty necessarily implies a process of liberation.
2. Cf. W. Pannenberg, *Basic Questions in Theology*, vol. 2, pp. 2-27, SCM Press Ltd, 1970.
3. Op. cit. p. 55.
4. *ENI Bulletin,* n°. 8, 25 April 1995.
5. S. Croatto, *Liberación y libertad*, Mundo Nuevo, Buenos Aires, 1973, pp. 27-61.
6. E. Fromm, *Escape from Freedom*, 1941.
7. One can see clearly the link between truth, freedom and love in Paul, in Galatians 5:13-15; and in Peter, in 1 Peter 1:17-22.

# CHILE

The continuing presence of General Augusto Pinochet on the margins of power casts a long shadow on the successive elected governments, since 1990, of Presidents Patricio Aylwin and Eduardo Frei. This state of affairs has curtailed severely their ability (and political will, according to numerous Chileans) to name those responsible for crimes against humanity and to prosecute military perpetrators. The freedom of movement enjoyed by insolent former torturers haunts the nightmares of Chilean victims, especially the women. Terrible and persistent effects of impunity are still experienced to a startling degree. In the mid-1990s, under intense political pressure from the USA, two high-ranking officers received comparatively light sentences for ordering the murder, in Washington D.C., of Salvador Allende's former foreign minister, Orlando Letelier. Despite the social impact of the 1993 publication of the report of the official Chile National Commission on Truth and Reconciliation, detailing the scope and nature of repression under military rule, the members of the armed forces and security police responsible for thousands of deaths by torture and political execution continue to go unpunished.

# BREAKING THE HUMAN LINK:
# THE MEDICO-PSYCHIATRIC VIEW OF IMPUNITY[1]

### *Paz Rojas Baeza*

## Introduction

The ideas that follow originated in the practical experience of providing comprehensive medical, psychological and social assistance to persons affected by the violence and the impunity granted to the military dictatorship in Chile (1973-90) and by the persistence of impunity after six years of transition to democracy (1990-95), during which time impunity was at its height.

One dictionary's definition of impunity is *exemption from punishment or penalty.* Amnesty – one of the mechanisms most frequently used to establish impunity – is derived from the word "amnesia", a medical term indicating the loss of memory, forgetting.

These meanings together with their consequences, make impunity a complex phenomenon pointing to one of the most dramatic aspects of human conduct. It represents an ambivalent combination of the will to know and judge, on the one hand, and the need to conceal and forget crimes committed, on the other.

The foundational ideas of the *polis* and of the State, which have for centuries defined relations between persons in society, were designed to maintain order and to provide sanctions. If order was not respected, punishment was meted out.

Over time, impunity has been addressed by various disciplines. Philosophy and the arts have discussed crimes and the need for punishment and responsibility, showing the tremendous significance of these concepts in human social relations. From their beginnings legal systems have dealt with these issues, but their frequent failure to enforce principles has often led to greater conflict.

The human tendency to avoid the concrete and obscure truth found its supreme expression in Latin America many years after the end of the Second World War. The period of the Cold War was marked by particularly gross violations of human rights: the denial of economic, social and cultural rights and the virtual elimination of protections of civil and political rights:

- persecution, raids, threats
- torture in secret places or in the open air
- detention and prolonged imprisonment
- large-scale exile, expatriation and banishments

- political crimes, summary executions, false confrontations,
- and one of the most dramatic crimes: kidnapping and disappearance which, since the 1970s alone, has claimed som 120,000 victims

Those years also saw the emergence of war councils, military tribunals, ordinary courts devoid of independence and impartiality, laws granting amnesty to those responsible, and laws of *Punto Final*, drawing a line under the past, in a futile attempt to make people forget.

After this period of military dictatorships – which are still in power in some Latin American countries – "democracies in transition" were installed. All of these grantied impunity to those responsible for crimes.

It is in this context that in Chile, months after the 1973 *coup d'etat*, we started treating individuals, families and small rural communities affected by the violence of the dictatorship.

After several years of hesitation faced with the tortured bodies and minds and with the aggression perpetrated consciously, and given the insufficiency of our concepts of health and illness, lacking therapeutic guidelines for dealing with the disorders, we finally concluded that all the people we were treating had been affected by two types of aggression: crimes against humanity, and impunity.

Over the years we have observed that these persons show no significant phenomenological differences – in terms of symptoms or syndromes – from other persons suffering medico-psychological disorders provoked by other factors.

We did observe, however, that in both groups of persons – those with secondary disorders in the wake of violation of their human rights, and those whose disorders were caused by other factors – the biographical factors, the personality make-up, as well as their beliefs and value systems, in short, their life history also played a role in the configuration of their disorders and in its evolution and prognosis.

The major difference between the two groups lies first and foremost in *the causes*, what originated and triggered the disorder – in medical terms, the etiology. In second place, the difference lies in the abnormal psychodynamics triggered by this etiology, and which lead to such disorders.

In trying to understand the illness and hence to decide how to approach and possibly treat it, we are breaking new ground, crossing uncharted terrain. Moreover, we have a scientific imperative to ensure the clarity of the hypothesis that we will be trying to substantiate in this paper: *over time, the presence of impunity becomes a mechanism of intra-psychic and intersubjective disturbance capable of provoking mental disorders which are at least as serious as those produced by torture. It therefore requires to be treated with the utmost human concern.*

## Initial attempt at clarification of terms

In very broad outlines, we may speak of two forms of impunity: impunity for the perpetrators of human rights violations, and the impunity which has come about as a historical continuum in Latin America. Here I refer to the grave and ongoing violations of economic, social and cultural rights of persons and peoples.

In our practice we deal mainly with the first type of impunity, though not without taking account of the impact of social, economic and cultural factors in shaping individuals. It bears upon their intra-family relations, their culture, and their own particular and unique way of being throughout their lives.

Impunity is a new aggression, above and beyond the crimes against humanity already committed. Added to the traumatic consequences of pain, suffering, loss, bereavement and helplessness experienced, impunity attacks major human values, destroys beliefs and principles and alters the norms and rules that humankind has gradually built up over time.

## The structure of impunity

We must understand impunity as an organized whole with its different component parts. Knowing the relationships arising from them will help us better to understand the *psychological disorders* caused by its different elements in individuals, families and in society.

Impunity is a human decision, an action, a behaviour, an act of denial of concrete reality: it is an act of violence. It is an instance of human aggression which, in addition to not being fully revealed, is also to be left unpunished.

At the heart and origin of impunity is a *crime*, which is the first thing that is to be concealed. This crime has one or several victims, and one or several authors. It was perpetrated at a particular place, in a precise geographical location, at a given time, on a particular day and date. In the minds of the victims, recollections of place and time sometimes seem a certainty and sometimes a figment of the imagination.

With impunity, the crime and its circumstances remain anonymous, shrouded in the silence of the unknown.

The crime is committed in a national and international historical, social and political context. If crimes against humanity were committed under a legal system of "State terrorism", the impunity guaranteed by the State during such a period would be a component factor which aided and abetted the crime. In such a case, the authors are the very persons who ordered or carried out the crime.

Impunity that extends into democracy or into a period of transition to democracy is different and, perhaps for that very reason, is experienced even more dramatically by its victims. In such a case, the human decision no longer resides in a tyrannical but in a democratic power, in which all the branches of State participate at different levels and with different degrees of involvement, approving and permitting it. It is the institutional structure that is compromised by the continuation of impunity.

The attitude of an apathetic, indifferent civil society seemingly disposed towards forgetting is perceived as equally aggressive. Conversely, a responsive attitude marked by commitment and receptivity does engender hope.

Also part of impunity, though at a more peripheral level, are the actions of regional or universal human rights institutions. What they do or fail to do, say or fail to say, what they reject or accept in the face of various impunity mechanisms such as amnesty laws, laws of *Punto Final*, expiry and the use of military courts also play a part in the hopes, wishes, frustrations and despair of the persons and families affected.

## Structure of the crime

Whoever says crime, has two things in mind: the person aggressed, killed or made to disappear, and the aggressor or perpetrator. The word crime bespeaks an indissoluble human link. With impunity, one of the actors in the crime, the person responsible, remains unknown in this human link. It may also be said that at a deeper level, this human link is produced through the exercise of a human passion: violence. Violence, which, in contrast to other passions, is solely destructive.

When confronted with the marks left by the violence of these crimes on the minds and bodies of people, we remembered what Freud wrote in 1915 in his article: "Thoughts for the Times on War and Death", "Two things (in this war) have evoked our sense of disillusionment: the destitution shown in moral relations externally by the states (which in their interior relations pose as guardians of accepted moral usage) and the brutality in behaviour shown by individuals..."

Undoubtedly, when confronted with these crimes, our first astonished question was: what type of violence were we dealing with, who had done it and what did it mean, both to those who had endured it and those who had applied it?

The problem we faced was having to assume that the violence which, among animals, is used only for defence or for procuring food and mates, had been unleashed in human beings for other very specific purposes which had nothing to do with these needs.

The term violence derives from the Classical Latin word *violentia,* the noun from the verb *violare.* It has its origin in the Greek *via,* which quite simply corresponds to the notion of vital force. Later, *violentia* in Latin and *violence* in French came to signify life, the life or survival instinct.

In this case, however, it had acquired the opposite meaning to that linked to life, for by taking the form of aggression and concealment, of destruction and death, violence had become the negation of life.

Ortega and Gasset described violence as "despairing reason", which we can understand in connection with the violence unleashed in response to a situation of oppression, privation, abandonment, where life is without hope and feels like confinement, like a punishment. That is *structural violence.* The violence of these crimes is very different, it emanates from the seat of power.

It has its own logic, which is not at all despairing. It has neither the anguish nor the helplessness of despair. Quite the contrary, the crime and the many ways of carrying it out are rationally studied and planned.

In this case, violence is used to establish political power, to maintain and make it work, but above all, to subdue the population by direct or indirect destruction through fear and terror.

In this form of violence, aggression, which covers all behaviours designed to inflict pain, wounds or destruction on another human being is compounded by the planning of the violence, the setting up of the apparatus of repression to apply it, the use of specific techniques and the training of specialized personnel to carry out the crime.

If we add impunity to this violence, the disorders produced within the victim, in interpersonal relations and in collective behaviour attain a dimension difficult to understand and evaluate.

With impunity, the details of the crime are not known, only the victims are known and, in the case of the disappeared, the crime is as much a certainty as it is an uncertainty. With impunity, the crime and its circumstances remain anonymous, shrouded in the silence of the unknown.

## Classification of the crimes

The outrage and consternation over the crimes committed by the Nazis during the Second World War produced the inescapable need to adopt measures of an international nature, binding on all humanity, to guard against such crimes.

It would not be appropriate for us, as physicians, to embark on a lengthy discussion of international law. Nevertheless, since all individuals, families and communities with whom we have worked are part of the totality of persons affected by the so-called crimes against humanity, we would like to offer some ideas on this subject, for the sake of a better understanding of its consequences and of why the perpetrators cannot be dissociated from their crimes.

One of the first things that the General Assembly of the United Nations did in 1946 was to define and classify crimes of this nature so as to prevent their recurrence and to punish those guilty of crimes against humanity. Two major forms of crimes were defined and classified: war crimes and crimes against humanity.

A process was then begun to elaborate official instruments condemning both types of crime. That process culminated in the drafting of two important conventions and a set of principles. The first convention was entitled *Convention on the Prevention and Punishment of the Crime of Genocide.* The second, addressing the inescapable need always to investigate and punish crimes against humanity regardless of time, was the *Convention on the Non-Applicability of Statutory Limitation to War Crimes and Crimes against Humanity.* The principles are entitled: *Principles of international cooperation in the detection, arrest, extradition and punishment of persons guilty of war crimes and crimes against humanity.*

Although every crime should be interpreted according to its own specifics, we would like to highlight what we perceive as elements of psychological importance in crimes against humanity.

Violence experienced by the persons we have treated is violence emanating from the seat of power, specifically from the state. In accordance with our medical practice, we would argue that it is *violence at its extreme*, in its highest form, produced by a system that engages the human being's most elevated faculty, that of reason, and is aimed at destroying in a fellow human being the very essence of what makes that being unique and irreplaceable.

In the case of a declared war between two or more countries, persons are free to decide to become combatants, indeed they may even do so because of an ideal, a cause, or necessity. Their situation vis-a-vis the enemy is, therefore, *one of equality*, at least as regards the will for power, and even though their forces may be in a situation of inferiority, it is a choice, their choice.

The situation is very different for persons who have lived under State terrorism for, in contrast to open or declared wars, the struggle of the individual is one of total and absolute *inequality with the other human being.*

What constitutes the specific nature of this crime is that the affected persons, as we have been told, are confronted with a completely new situation, not of their own choosing, never before experienced, pervaded by violence, aggression and at the same time concealment. Such a situation has no precedent, it cannot be associated with any memory, it has no verifiable mental representation.

Thus we have a triad – the person responsible, the victim and the relationship established between them – in which the persecuted, tortured or disappeared person, in short, the victim, is helpless, defenceless, most of the time tied up, blindfolded, naked and deprived of all human dignity. In contrast, the perpetrator is in full possession of his/her faculties and destructive power, is subject to no time constraints, and can therefore inflict physical and mental suffering, leading to the disintegration of a fellow and similar human being, who has been transformed into the enemy.

Violence and aggression are the human interaction that links them. The relationship that arises between them is perverse.

We shall now try to break down this relationship so as to identify what impunity conceals with respect to the crime and to try to understand this complex human act.

### Those responsible

Because of impunity, we have come to know the profile of the person responsible, only through the survivors. They told us of profoundly traumatic experiences which they were unable for the most part to put into words.

Of all the persons treated by us, some one thousand men and women underwent torture. They had been face to face with, and at the mercy of their torturer.

In addition, the image of the perpetrator also appears in the imagination and the fantasy of relatives of victims of political killings and missing detainees. Some 200 family members make up this group.

But despite the haunting memory, the constant representation and the undeniable presence of the perpetrator in society, the granting of impunity is the supreme expression of *the way in which we as human beings arrange not to know.*

Numerous national and international studies, some done with rigorous method and based on vast research concerning military training, strategies, techniques of interrogation and torture, training to defeat the enemy, have systematized the sociological, ideological and political mechanisms used to transform someone into a torturer or murderer.

## "Torturing is taught and learned"

Freud, in his famous reply to Einstein, who had asked him about the reason for war, said: "Because man is what he is", adding nonetheless some years later, that undoubtedly his reply had been "sterile and unsatisfactory". Finding the answer to that question contitutes the major challenge now facing psychology, ethics and the humanities in general.

Throughout our clinical experience, understanding the psycho-pathological mechanisms of impunity and pinpointing their severe consequences were *central to efforts to forestall* the disorders caused by these crimes. Within the scope of this preventive action, identifying the perpetrator, in addition to being a therapeutic factor, came to represent a major ethical challenge that had the effect of stabilizing intense emotions.

This is why, from the medico-psychological-ethical point of view, the present attitude of behaving "as if nothing had happened", as if the *parillas* (electrified bedsprings), the clandestine locations and the disappearances had not existed, is unacceptable.

## First level

Working and furthermore living in a country under dictatorship, we quickly assumed that responsibility was spread over different levels, both in executing and concealing the crime.

The problem is that, in relation to impunity in transition periods, the number of persons responsible by commission or by omission increases. Such persons are located within the institutional structures themselves.

Responsibility lies, therefore, with the person who plans, conceals and denies, who detains, kidnaps, tortures and causes to disappear. That person digs graves, moves bodies, makes them vanish. Hundreds of persons perform these acts. Yet, the perpetrator remains in the realm of the unknown, hence does not exist as a tangible person.

It would perhaps be useful to our study to start by recounting the Chilean experience. Of the hundreds of men and women involved – who, according to Pinochet's Chief of Political Police, Manuel Contreras, numbered over 50,000 civil servants – two junior secret service officers, from the Army and the Air Force, have related their macabre experiences. Neither did so publicly. One spoke from the country where he took refuge and the other in private with a journalist, after which he left the country secretly on account of harassment. A third perpetrator who broke the silence almost 10 years after the 1973 *coup d' état* was murdered by unknown persons.

All the others have kept silent and they have acknowledged nothing. Despite the incredible offers of guaranteed anonymity and protection, they have not contributed a single iota of background information.

The perpetrator therefore is a non-existent character, an absent member. Nevertheless, traces of his/her crimes have been left on the minds and bodies of the persons aggressed or in clandestine cemeteries, but these are scenes without authors, without movement, without attitudes or where an important element is missing, in short, scenes for which no-one is responsible.

Those responsible are real persons. They have last names and given names. They maintain interpersonal relationships with other members of society, with their families. Impunity allows them to be among us.

Impunity deprives us of the principal part of the equation of the act which violates the right to life. It remains unrevealed: the figure of the author of the crime. That figure therefore necessarily turns into an infinite and infernal symbolic representation.

The author crystallizes the exogenous factor in the renewed "*pathos*" which acts on any individual, in the whole society. The perpetrator comes to incarnate power transformed into despotic power.

We came to know the perpetrators, as we have said, only through the accounts of the survivors. When they were able to see them they retained distinct recollections of their bodies, faces and gestures; their penetrating stares that distilled coldness and hatred; their insults, their thick, moist and lascivious lips. Their permanent scowls of contempt and scorn were remembered time and time again by our patients. Where the torture victims had been blindfolded and could not see their torturers, they recall "the tough, fat, hot, depraved hands" that struck them. Their memories reverberate with degrading and scornful words, contemptuous phrases "which cannot be forgotten, which never go away and which keep coming back time and time again, words of hatred and humiliation". They hear a "voice that jeers, shouts, shrieks, and penetrates so deeply as to pierce the eardrums and the soul". It is a voice that changes direction, place and tone, "one that you never stop hearing". Words, repeated phrases, always in their memories, indelibly imprinted, "he told me, he shouted at me, he threatened me". Together with these memories, the acts inflicting pain and trauma with blows, electrodes, hoses, machines, knives, and other intruments become an ever-present backdrop. The figure of the perpetrator becomes a vivid image and influences latent behaviour for life.

From early on we managed to draw up a bio-psycho-ideological profile of some of the perpetrators who were repeatedly described.

We would like to present some of these elements concerning present-day perpetrators in different Latin American countries. While this knowledge is the result of a medical imperative of getting to know the etiology of disorders, it is also fundamentally the product of a compelling concern with ethics and prevention.

The perpetrator of the crime is someone who freely uses his/her reason, who acts in a lucid and conscious manner and who moreover perceives his/her crime as a necessity, a duty, and as an act of good.

What goes into forming such a person, whose conduct is totally governed by obedience?

What Foucault calls a "new technology of the self" had been created whereby, in contrast to the old obedience of monks who sacrificed self and personal desire to God, the sacrifice is now offered to those in power.

We used the paradigms of the Cold War in order to arrive at this interpretation. Many documents on national security have described the genesis of the idea of the permanent and constant existence of an enemy: the enemy that is within each country and is thereby the "internal enemy".This enemy became "the communist, the subversive, the red, the terrorist...", descriptives used by the perpetrators as they tortured their victims.

**How the perpetrators were trained**

Not only were Latin American military personnel given a Manichean view of the world, but it was also deeply inculcated into them that they constituted "an exclusive world set apart from the rest of society". Their minds were subjected to a rigid ideological brainwashing process.

They developed feelings of impunity, omnipotence, of being in command over others, of contempt and repugnance for the adversary.

While the enemy was dehumanized, they became accustomed to cruelty and to automatic obedience. The were promised power and absolute impunity.

Throughout this process, they internalized a symbolic discourse: torturing, killing and making people disappear is to defend a just cause. They believed that they had a certain mission as saviours, in which their ideals were superior to those of the civil society.

This dual message made it possible for the victim to be transformed into the culprit of the tragedy.

Furthermore, on the basis of handbooks on psychological warfare, specialized material on the training of Latin American military personnel in schools in the United States (Brazilians, Chileans, Argentinians and Guatemalans), of documents found in the archives of the Paraguayan dictatorship and even in training handbooks existing in the libraries of South American armies, we concluded that *the psychological stratagem used to indoctrinate and mould the behaviour of the perpetrators is the constant manipulation of the mechanisms of fear.*

Fear of the other, terror of the "internal enemy", who, if not eliminated, if not killed, will kill them instead. If not destroyed, the enemy will seize power. It is a deep-seated, internalized fear, covered in this case by uniforms and ranks, but it is basically perhaps the same fear felt by primitive man, the hunter, *vis-à-vis* wild beasts.

Many studies also suggest that human aggression in the form of violence is an integral part of our make-up. If this is so, the problem then becomes one of knowing how it was honed and taken to the extreme in some persons, who do not hesitate to use it and then deny it afterwards.

Were it not for impunity, we would be trying to dismantle such special formative mechanisms, and starting instead to rebuild the ethics of fundamental human dignity.

## Breaking the human link

In a study we recently conducted on persons tortured more than 10 years ago, we found that one of the most intense and persistent disorders was the relationship established between themselves and the aggressor during torture sessions. What recurred and persisted in their recollections was the ever-impending arrival of the interrogators and torturers. They have not forgotten this, neither have they forgotten their aggressors' desire to destroy them, their need to delve "into the innermost aspects of our lives".

In a detailed study of the disorders displayed by these persons following torture, we found that a link of distrust had been gradually formed in all of them. We concluded that there was a dual mechanism at work in creating this distrust: On the one hand, there was the loss of self-esteem on account of the disintegration of the self induced by torture; and the on other, the difficulty of interacting with other people. This was caused, in turn, by the lack of trust in human beings engendered by the interaction with the torturer. We advanced the theory that *the nature of their inter-subjectivity had been radically altered.*

This was so because all that a human being does, thinks and creates from birth onwards is part of a process of interchange with the other. This means that conduct is always a link. It is dictated by behaviours deriving from interpersonal relations.

The frame of reference of all mental and physical activity is "experience" with another party, be it an animate object – a person – or an inanimate object.

Therefore, all our behaviours *vis-à-vis* objects or persons encountered for the first time are largely influenced or conditioned by the process of experience – or knowledge we had in previous relationships with other persons or objects: in other words, from all that constitutes the human link as such. The term link is applied to the entire structure built up by the subject, namely, the self, the object or other, and the quality of the relationship established between both.

Throughout life, the other, or whatever is represented by that other, is gradually internalized and remains as a mark or imprint that may even be unconscious. This is what is known in psychoanalysis as the "virtual object". That is to say, it is not present but has been internalized and can reemerge in forms and expressions that go beyond our rational and conscious will.

We wish to underline that in the triad previously mentioned as aspects of impunity worthy of study (the person responsible, the victim and the link between them), *the interpersonal relationship and the psychological mechanisms activated by these relations are doubly pathological.*

Under normal circumstances the human link is usually formative, a means of transmitting affection, knowledge and practices. It is a vehicle for the formation of values, plans, ideals and, over time, for constructing mostly positive memories.

In contrast, in the relationship created with the torturer (in the case of survivors), or the imagined event (in the case of family members of disappeared or executed detainees), the role of the link is the inverse. It is perverted, destructive and over time becomes a sinister memory that damages subsequent relations with other people. The memory of the relationship with the torturer destroys the person inwardly, as s/he relives in a vivid and destructive manner the scenes of torture and his/her attitude to the torturers.

In effect, the link established between the torturer and the victim is indelibly imprinted on the victim's mind. The actions of the torturer, the torture and punishment meted out at the corporal, sensory and cognitive levels abruptly interrupt the psychological experience-gathering process reaching back to earlier interaction with other persons. This process could be altered for life, especially when there is impunity.

## Sequels in the person

What disorders were suffered by the people we treated, as a result of impunity? What psychopathological mechanisms were triggered by it? What role did its existence and its duration in time play in shaping clinical patterns?

All life is jointly determined by the inner neuropsychological world and the external surrounding world, in a dialectic process.

Existence is shaped for each person by the development of knowledge, subjectivity and the formation of values – within clear frames of reference. How people become aware of things determines how they act. We can observe the historical, cultural and social synthesis which individuals represent. Learning accumulated over centuries is transmitted through interaction with other human beings, with whom a person exchanges experiences, feelings, knowledge and practices. Life is thus a constant polemic with the world and with reality. Everyday life and relationships create each individual's system of values and principles, and constitutes the basis of knowledge, affectivity and behaviour. Of prime importance as axiological guidelines are, among others, the categories of what is good and what is evil, the true and the false, the just and the unjust, the sacred and the profane.

Truth, objectivity as the structural foundation of reality, is an essential element in the whole process by which we understand and know. Certainty about what is true and what is false is essential to the formation of judgment, reason, thought and affectivity. Certainty about what is real or unreal is the basis on which all mental functions develop: in language, ideas, reason, conscience, as well as sensations, affectivity and subjectivity.

During the therapy process, we realized from what people told us that the external world is profoundly altered by the existence of impunity. The surrounding world becomes false and alien as well as threatening. The parameters of reality are altered and distorted by concealment and deceit.

Impunity falsifies the "material" which knowledge assimilates, analyses and synthesizes. Consequently, without truth it is impossible to construct a stable inner world. On the contrary, the whole of life is invaded by doubt and distrust. It unleashes disruptive dynamics, traced to the disequilibrium and bewilderment produced by impunity. *The realm of subjectivity disintegrates, human relations become perverted and permeated by fear.*

With impunity, knowing becomes confused, submerged, hidden, and uncertain. Attacks against life remain  unexplained for ever. This creates fear, anxiety and guilt, which elicit abnormal responses and behaviour. *Uncertainty enters the psyche.*

Just as important are feelings and the perception of what is just or unjust – the feeling through which ideas are formed and behaviour is programmed.

Closely linked to these feelings is the need to give credit to the one who was not at fault, and to sanction or punish the one who was, the one who transgressed the rules.

Moral rules have to be based on truth to be socially constructed. They have to be in line with what is judged to be just. Appropriate sanctions have to be applied, when what has been done does not correspond to what has been defined as socially, culturally and affectively correct over the centuries.

*The parameters of justice and punishment are thus central axes on which the behaviour of individuals has been constructed and societies based; states have been created and developed with rules, laws and norms. Impunity transgresses against all these parameters and consequently produces a major conflict of feelings.*

The absence of truth and justice is infininitely more serious when that which is unknown and unprosecuted has to do with the problem of life and death. Worse still, not knowing whether a person is alive and not knowing what might have happened (as in the case of the families of detainees who disappeared) carries with it all the emotional burden of alienation, horror, imagination and memories.

When what happened – and is still happening – is not known, we find an extreme, boundary situation, the more painful and dangerous when those responsible for it are known to know the truth but deny and conceal it.

A feeling of anger at the repeated demonstrations of impunity from punishment, added to prolonged suffering and unresolved grief and alienation, leads to a sense of disbelief and disgust. The suffering caused by these crimes cannot be considered as a single event which took place at a specific time. The torture, killing or disappearance of a relative are continuing events. Although they started at a given place and time, in the microcosm of the torture chambers or the death scenarios they continue to be played out unendingly in all spheres of a person's life, especially in his /her relations with others and links with society. Time is experienced and perceived as infinite when impunity persists.

Freud was of the opinion that "dangers came from three sources: from the instincts, from moral consciousness and from external reality". In these cases it is precisely external reality which has turned into a danger. The disorders of which these people suffer are not primarily physical or organic in origin. They are caused by external aggressions, the secondary effect of which is to harm the person's self.

Furthermore, impunity alters moral consciousness. However in this case the disorder derives principally from the external world because when norms and values are turned upside-down by official institutions these challenge and contradict feelings and behaviour. On the other hand, conflicting doubts and impulses stemming from the person's own desire for revenge and feelings of guilt challenge personal morality.

Among the persons we treated it is even possible to draw up a pathological classification, as has been done in international classifications of mental illnesses. In our experience, however, they are unique and specific in each individual case, depending on the significance each person attaches to the aggression, depending on how each one resisted or did not resist the violence, on the relationship established with the torturer, on the feelings aroused in each one by the denials, lying, concealment and injustice and on the sense of abandonment, persecution and vulnerability that develops *vis-à-vis* the authorities.

These disorders cannot be classified by symptoms or syndromes; their specificity lies in their origin, their etiology. What triggers off the psychodynamic processes described in the production of the disorders is behaviour which aggresses and contradicts human life and community at every level.

## Sequels in the family

Death or the threat of death is an event which can disrupt a family. A family unit is in *functional equilibrium* when it experiences a calm period in which each one of its members functions with a reasonable degree of efficiency. In face of the loss – physical, functional and emotional – of one of its members, the intensity of the emotional reaction depends on the functional importance of the person who dies, the role he or she occupied in the family structure; the life cycle of the family, the grief work they are able to do, their participation in the search for truth and justice and the recognition of their truth by their immediate circle and by society.

The political repression and the crimes committed were directed against organized groups of people in the political, social and trade union sphere. But in the last analysis, the damage was done to *individual people who were part of a family.*

The acts of repression which affected families suddenly and tragically interrupted a balance (achieved over the years), a particular dynamic among its members, a special form of affective relationships and communication. The hierarchical structure was disrupted, leading to a realignment of the family structure as it sought to adapt to the loss of one of its members and face up to the act of repression.

This readaptation, being functional in the circumstances, served as a defence mechanism to provide for security and survival and avoid the breakdown of the individuals and the family in face of paralysis and fear.

The families achieved a new type of structure with varying degrees of stability, despite the presence of more or less pathological relations in their mode of functioning.

The time a family needs to establish a new emotional balance depends on its previous emotional integration and the intensity of the traumatic event. A well-integrated family may show a serious reaction at the time and then adapt. A less well integrated one may show a less obvious reaction at the time, but then respond over a longer period with symptoms of physical or emotional illness, or atypical social behaviour by all or some of its members.

In face of the crime and the inability to understand why, how, and whom, there were two general types of response by a family:

• *Isolation and withdrawal* individually and as a family, leading basically to the "privatization" of grief: the family experiences the death as belonging purely to its private sphere as though it were a natural or accidental death, and is unable to set it in a socio-political context. On the one hand, this creates feelings of guilt at not having cared enough for the person, not having had a closer or better relationship with him or her, or not having spent more time with him. On the other hand, because they are not able to vent their anger and their feelings of impotence, fear or distress at the event and are unable to validate them by sharing them with others, those feelings are turned inwards against the self in the form of self-hatred and depression. Within the family, inner tensions produce friction, clashes and arguments. Repeated in both the personal and the family sphere, these in turn generate serious dysfunctioning: crisis, division and break-up of the family.

• A second, more organized form of response is *grouping together* in human rights and/or family organizations. This has enabled some families to make sense of their grief, to channel their anger in a more constructive direction and to demand justice for the victims. This form of response has also generated chronic conflicts within families because of the different roles assumed by their members, thereby limiting their repertory of behaviour.

Whatever type of response families have managed to give, the thing that has not been possible – except in some exceptional cases – is to find out the whole truth about what happened.  The fact that any hope of those responsible for their situation being brought to justice seems further away today than ever before, has left them as *helpless victims of impunity.* Consequently, they cannot heal the damage and are unable to move forward into the future as an autonomous family group.

We may note at least six dynamics at work in families in response to crime and impunity: denial and isolation; identification with death; guilt; displacement of the social and the private; confusion; and lastly, reaction formation.  These six dynamics are superimposed on one another and are hard to observe separately.  However, they can be identified and detected at work within families when their different members display one or several of these forms of reaction in response to their loss.

The disorders we have observed in families as a result of the crimes and impunity are thus translated in their external relations as:

- social isolation, as a group and also of some of its members
- marginalization
- distrust of those around them, with serious difficulties in creating new social ties
- withdrawal from political life
- absence of plans for the future

*Within the family* the effects appear as:

- insecurity about everyday life and the future
- difficulty in establishing good communication within the family
- rigidity of intra-family relationships (clustered families) or almost total lack or break-up of relationships (scattered families)
- rigidity of boundaries *vis-à-vis* the world outside the family, difficulty in admitting others (friends, acquaintances, partners, political family, etc.)
- rigidity of hierarchy
- feelings of worthlessness on the part of various family members
- constant fear that "something" unspecified may happen to any of its members, apprehensiveness, and over-protectiveness
- difficulty in handling the changes connected with the transition to the different family life cycles, which are seen as a threat to its integrity
- restraint, repression or denial of feelings that are seen as "negative" (grief, sorrow and anger) or unacceptable in terms of their scale of values
- transmission of instability, despair, distrust and fear to new family members

Struggling against impunity represents a new *intrusion into the structure acquired by the family*. It gives new meaning to the traumatic event and, in many cases, once again places the criminal act and the loss at the heart of the family dynamic. With impunity, this new balance is broken, causing new cycles of serious disorders to start all over again in face of the contradictory, paradoxical behaviour and denials on the part of the state and its institutions.

## Sequels in society

What effects does the existence of crimes against humanity, long concealed by impunity, have on society?

They make themselves felt in a direct, open and generalized form in the behaviour of civil society and the State. It makes them all the more distressing. However, it is not possible to assess this objectively because their effects are immeasurable.

For some people, principally sociologists, society is the main source of morality, and it is precisely within society that impunity produces an ethical breakdown.

It does so because without truth and justice, ethics gradually disintegrates, producing, as we have noted, a continuous break in personal life and life in community with others. This ethical breakdown which started with the dictatorships was carried over into the period of transition with the continued existence of impunity.

It is in society that the two different forms of impunity are indissolubly combined. In the first of these, linked to structural violence, violence is historically inherent in the Latin American situation. Impunity is concretely expressed in the form of social injustice. In the second, connected with the crimes, it is expressed through the absence of truth and of justice.

We shall mention some elements of social injustice. This, because a large portion of the people we have cared for belong to the most needy and deprived sectors of society. The effects of these two forms of impunity were dramatically combined for these people after the military coup. In the case of social injustice, the truth is visible and cannot be denied. It is evident in the extreme poverty which engulfs large areas of this continent.

Neo-liberal policies applied in Latin America, and specifically in Chile – while reducing inflation – have increased the number of poor people in this continent, and the gap between the rich and the poor has grown steadily wider.

The lack of security and of opportunity, destitution and neglect have diminished the humanizing role which government should play. It also ushered in serious disturbances, reflected in the following social pathologies – rural migration to the cities; the murder of street children; human degradation and prostitution; street and domestic violence; vandalism; drug addiction and alcoholism. In short, all the manifestations of human deprivation – promiscuity, illiteracy, isolation, withdrawal, speech disturbance or mutism and torment. While studying the consequences of impunity among the families of executed political prisoners and missing detainees in two regions in the south of Chile, we found that the combination of these two forms of impunity is the true etiology of the serious disorders presented by these people.

In one way or another, the whole of society knew about the use of torture and the disappearances. Psychological warfare ensured that the *collective reign of terror necessary to maintain power* was stepped up. Consequently a deep-seated, though largely sub-conscious fear took hold of society. Some people recognized the facts; most denied them. Nonetheless, people's minds were constantly haunted by ideas and images of torture and death. A kind of morbid fantasy entered the popular consciousness. The crime perpetrated by human violence thus spread throughout society. It penetrated deeply into subjectivity and became permanently engraved in the collective unconscious.

In these circumstances, defence mechanisms of denial developed to block knowledge, precipitating a break with reality and the need to block feelings. Individualism increased.

Withdrawal and self-absorbtion, distrust and social fragmentation characterized some small mountain communities in which we worked.

The Government failed to react to the violations, to identify those responsible, to reveal the truth and to bring them to justice. It made it possible to justify violence and the use of violence, as a consequence.

What meaning can the values of right and wrong now have in the life of society? With impunity, the whole structure of civil responsibility has collapsed beyond repair, producing a *dissociated communal life in society: knowing yet concealing, being informed but keeping quiet; wanting to forget yet remembering; seeking good but doing wrong; wanting to be conciliating and rebelling.*

The two forms of impunity, described above, with the respective mechanisms we have mentioned, have turned into an ongoing trauma in society.

The programme of the first transition government literally stated the following: "The democratic government will undertake to establish the truth in the cases of violations of human rights which have occurred since the eleventh of September 1973. It will likewise endeavour to bring to trial, under the terms of criminal law, the violations of human rights involving atrocities against human life, freedom and personal integrity." Such was the ethical content of the discourse about national reconciliation.

The governement promised "to repeal the procedural rules established under the present regime which place obstacles in the way of judicial investigation or establish arbitrary privileges favouring state officials who may have been involved in the violations of human rights."

It stated that "in no case can the State refrain from penal action, without prejudice to the right of individuals concerned to exercise their own rights." The Decree-Law on Amnesty was challenged. "By its legal nature and true meaning and scope, the DL on Amnesty of 1978 cannot and shall not be an obstacle to establishing the truth, investigating the facts and determining criminal responsibilities and consequent sanctions in cases of crimes against human rights, such as detention followed by disappearance, crimes against life and the inflicting of serious physical or psychological wounds. The democratic government will promote the repeal or annulment of the Decree-Law on Amnesty."

There was consensus agreement on the need to establish the truth on what had happened. Once the new government was elected, as in other Latin American countries, the so-called Truth Comissions were set up to clarify the situation, known in Chile as the Commission on Truth and Reconciliation.

One of the recommendations made by this Commission was on the subject of truth: "Establishing the truth is not only a preventive measure in itself but also the basic prerequisite for any other preventive measures that may finally be adopted. If truth is to fulfil its preventive function there are certain minimum requirements to be respected, i.e. it must be impartial, full and objective so that it can create certainty in the national consciousness about how the events took place and how they unduly affected the honour and dignity of the victims."

In respect of reconciliation it was noted that justice was essential: "From the strictly preventive point of view, this Commission considers that an essential element in achieving national reconciliation and so avoiding any repetition of the events which occurred would be for the state to exercise its punitive powers to the full..." adding thereafter "we consider it necessary to punish those who conceal this kind of information..."

The report of the Commission on Truth and Reconciliation undoubtedly represented a step forward in the quest for truth. It became official. But even so that truth was incomplete, curtailed. The list of victims was not accompanied by a list of culprits – an empty space, a blank page in the eyes of society.

Moreover, in the case of Chile, torture – the main weapon used by the dictatorship to destroy and subdue – was excluded from the Commission's mandate of investigation. On the other hand, infringing upon the basic principle of international law which says that violations of human rights are acts concerning only states, crimes caused by political violence arising in response to the dictatorship, were included.

The Commission considered only a few cases where there were adequate grounds for trial, but privately. Neither society at large, nor even in some cases the family, were informed of these proceedings.

When the Commission's Report was published all the branches of the Armed Forces repudiated it. They denied the crimes and arrogantly proclaimed their version of the truth. No-one refuted the findings of the report. Little by little, demands were scaled down. Political discourse and ideological confrontation confused the population. Messages were sent out to the effect that "justice will be done as far as possible".

A change started to take place in language and meaning: the terrorists were not the people who committed the violations of human rights. Impunity was called reconciliation; the persistence of dictatorial power was transition; the oppressors were democrats; the crimes were excesses; arbitrary power was the rule of law.

A discourse was built up on false suppositions: to safeguard democracy you must sacrifice human rights; to find the truth, justice must be abandoned; to know the truth, the guilty must be protected; to achieve reconciliation, only the remains are to be found.

This kind of behaviour and discourse in the democracies-in-transition aggravate the existing social pathology, by adding scepticism, lack of meaning, anomy and deep-seated feelings of frustration and despair. That is why, important as it is to find the remains of those who disappeared and to heal the effects of torture, it is even more important to discover those who are responsible and to do justice.

## NOTE

1.  This article, written specifically for this series, was also published, in the original Spanish, as a contribution to the book *Persona, Estado, Poder: Estudios sobre Salud Mental*, Vol. II. Santiago de Chile: CODEPU, May 1996. It will appear later in German in a publication of the *Nürnbuerger Menschenrechtszentrum* (Fürther Str. 22, 90429 Nürnberg, Germany). The paper was prepared in cooperation with the Mental Health Team DIT-T (Reporting, Investigation and the Treatment of Torture Victims and Their Family Nucleus) of the Committee for the Defence of the People's Rights (CODEPU), a human rights organization in Chile, which was assisted in this task by jurists, educators and human rights workers. The author thanks Veronica Seeger for her contribution to the Chapter entitled "Sequels in the family", and very especially, Victor Espinosa, who read the paper and made suggestions for greater clarity. The author states that "We are aware that the language of the paper falls between the 'scientific' and the highly subjective because in dealing with the subject we have become deeply involved with it. The bibliography provided includes only some of the texts that helped to enrich our work".

# BIBLIOGRAPHY

**Adorno, Th**. *Consignas: La Educación después de Auschwitz.* Buenos Aires: Amorrotu Editores, 1993.

**Amati, Silvia.** *Algunas Reflexiones sobre la Tortura para Introducir una Dimensión Psicoanalítica.* Ginebra: Mimeo, 1975.

**Amnesty International.** *La Torture: instrument de pouvoir, fléau à combattre.* Paris: Seuil, 1984.

**Barudy, J.; Serrano, J.; Marten, S.J.** *Los Problemas Psicológicos Provocados por la Tortura en los Refugiados Políticos Latinoamericanos.* Bruxelles: COLAT, 1980.

**Becker, David.** *Trauma, Duelo de Identidad: una reflexión conceptual.* Santiago: CESOC, 1994.

**Bergueret, Jean**. *La violence et la vie psycholgique* . Paris: Payot, 1994.

**Bettelheim, Bruno**. *The Informed Heart: Autonomy in a Mass Age.* Chicago: Free Press, 1960.

**Bettelheim, Bruno** and **Karlin, Daniel.** *Un autre regard sur la folie.* Paris: Stock, 1975.

**Bleuler, Eugen**. *Affektivität, Suggestibilität, Paranoia.* Halle: 1906.

**CODEPU-DITT.** *Persona, Estado, Poder: Estudio sobre salud mental, Chile 1973-1989.* Santiago de Chile: noviembre de 1989.

**CODEPU-DITT.** Seminário Internacional, *Tortura, Aspectos Médicos, Psicológicos y Sociales. Prevención y Tratamiento.* Santiago de Chile: 1989.

**Clastres, P.** *Archéologie de la violence libre.* Paris: Petite Bibliothèque Payot, 1977.

**Comblin, Joseph.** *Le pouvoir militaire en Amérique latine: l'idéologie de la securité nationale.* Paris: J.P. Delarge, 1977.

**D.S.M. III.** *Manual Diagnóstico y Estadístico de los Trastornos Mentales.* Paris: Edición Masson, 1983.

**Diez, Guinea**. "Guatemala, el país del Miedo". Guatemala City: En la *Revista Cronica,* 23 de septiembre de 1995.

**Freud, Sigmund.** *Neurose und Psychose.* Internationale Zeitschrift für ärztliche Psychoanalyse, 1924.

**Foucault, Michel.** *Naissance de la clinique: une archéologie du regard médical.* Paris: Presses universitaires de France, 1978.

**Garréton, Roberto**. *Amnistía y Reconciliación.* Mimeo. Santiago de Chile: 1995.

**Jacques, André**. *L'interdit ou la torture en procés.* Paris: Les Editions du Cerf, 1994.

**Le Shan, Lawrence**. *La Psicología de la Guerra: un estudio de su mística y su locura*. Santiago de Chile: Editorial Andrés Bello, 1995.

**Maffesoli, Michel**. *Essais sur la violence*. Paris: Librairie des Méridiens, 1954.

**Michaud, Ives**. *La Violence*. Paris: Presses universitaires de France, 1986.

**Moch, Anne**. *Les stress de l'environment*. Saint Denis/Paris: Presses universitaires de France, 1989.

*Chile: Recuerdos de la Guerra*, in the collection *Verdad Justicia*, Vol. II. Santiago de Chile: CODEPU, 1991.

**Montealegre, Hernán**. *Los Derechos Humanos en su Perspectiva Internacional*. Documento. Santiago de Chile: Comisión Chilena de Derechos Humanos, 1987.

**Puget, J., Kaes, R., Vignar, M**. *Violencia de Estado y Psicoanálisis*. Buenos Aires: Ed. Dunot & Coll, Inconsciente y Cultura, 1989.

**Reszczynski, K., Rojas, P., Barceló, P**. *Torture et résistance au Chili*. Paris: L'Harmattan, 1984.

**Rojas, Paz**. *Horror y Olvido*. Santiago de Chile: Mimeo, 1994.

**Rojas, Paz**. *"Impunidad y Salud Mental"*, en *Tortura*. Documento de Denuncia, Volumen IX. Santiago de Chile: CODEPU, 1989.

**Rojas, Paz**. "Introducción al Tratamiento y Rehabilitación de las Víctimas", en *Prevenir la Tortura: un desafío realista*. Ginebra: Association pour la Prévention de la Torture (APT), 1995.

**Serrano Rubio María Eugenia**. *Mémoire, consequences médico-psychologiques de la torture*. Doctoral thesis, mimeo. Paris: juin, 1991.

**Sveaass, Nora.** "Justicia y Reconciliación: los efectos psicológicos de la impunidad". In *Dolor y Sobrevivencia: Violaciones de Derechos Humanos y Salud Metal*, by Lavik, Nygard and Sveaass, Fannemel. Stockholm: Scandinavia University Press, 1994.

**Ulriksen de Viñar, Maren**. *"L'efficacité symbolique de la torture"*, dans *Solidarités et responsabilités face à la torture: Actes du Colloque de Strasbourg*, 2-3 septembre de 1994. Paris: Document ACAT.

**Vallejos, J., Ruiloba**. *Introducción a la Psicopatología y la Psiquiatría*. Salvat Editores, S.A., 1991.

**Viñar, Marcelo**. *Pedro y la Demolición*. Mimeo, 1975.

# A CHRISTIAN REFLECTION:
# WHAT WE SEE, THINK AND FEEL

### *Ecumenical Coordinating Assembly*

> *"Blessed are those who hunger and thirst*
> *for righteousness" (Mt.5:6)*

**What we see**

There have been several serious attempts to halt the investigations undertaken in Chile to establish the truth about violations of human rights, and to prevent those responsible from having to face justice. The ethical reasons given for attempting to justify forgetting the crimes against humanity perpetrated in the period from 1973-1990 and allowing them to go unpunished concern the need to achieve "reconciliation" in Chilean society, as a precondition for the country's peace and stability.

The starting point for the present negotiations was the blackmail exercised by the military following the sentencing of two members of the armed forces implicated in the murder of former Foreign Minister, Orlando Letelier. This attitude threatened national cohesion and infringed the very Constitution which they themselves had imposed on the country in 1980. It also showed the organic links between the political and economic Right and the Military Regime, and revealed the severe limitations and weaknesses of the present democratic order.

With civil society and its organizations as spectators, an intensive round of negotiations and agreements is being conducted among the governing elite, the Right and the Armed Forces. Everything seems to indicate that the intention is to turn the page on the crimes and, using legally novel formulas, to impose impunity.

It is disquieting that President Eduardo Frei's proposals concerning human rights emphasized exclusively the establishment of the truth, to the detriment of justice. The current legislative intitatives are a step forward when compared to the proposals of the previous government (the so-called "Aylwin Law"). But they are a step backwards as regards implementing justice.

It is also a matter for grave concern that the President of the Republic declined to consult the views of the Association of the Families of the Detained and Disappeared since the families are obviously the ones who suffered the full force of violations of human rights which occurred during the military dictatorship.

Equally disturbing is the narrow spectrum of political opinion consulted during the round of conversations held by the government before it announced its legislative proposals. All of the groups of the Chilean Left have been excluded. That section of the national community had been the direct target of the violations of human rights.

It seems inadmissible, in ethical terms, to try to link laws on constitutional reform, and on the armed forces, with measures pertinent to the problem of human rights, as though the democratization of the country depended on restricting the truth and circumventing justice. A democratic system built on such a basis would be meaningless.

## What we think and feel

Nothing that concerns human beings can be a matter of indifference to Christians. Shortly before he departed, our Lord prayed to the Father for his disciples "I am not asking you to take them out of the world, but I ask you to protect them from the evil one" (Jn 17:15).

Seen in this light, the defence of human rights is a central concern in our practice of the faith. We know that the infringement of human dignity is a direct and explicit offence against God himself (Matt. 25:40 and 45; Proverbs 19:17). Also "Is not this the fast that I choose: to loose the bonds of injustice, to undo the thongs of the yoke, to let the oppressed go free and to break every yoke?" (Isa. 58:6).

Those who set forth ideological and Christian ethical reasons to forget and to justify appeals for "forgiveness" and "reconciliation" are making a serious mistake.

This attempt to link reconciliation with impunity was rigorously denounced by God's prophets: "They have treated the wound of my people carelessly, saying 'Peace, peace,' when there is no peace" (Jeremiah 6:14), because "the effect of righteousness will be peace, and the result of righteousness, quietness and trust for ever" (Isaiah 32:1 and 17); James 3:18). Therefore, "There is no peace, says my God, for the wicked" (Isa. 57:21; 48:22).

Justice is not negotiable. Nor can it be reconciled with impunity: "...For what partnership is there between righteousness and lawlessness? Or what fellowship between is there between light and darkness?" (2 Cor. 6:14-15); "The children of God and the children of the devil are revealed in this way: all who do not do what is right are not from God" ( 1 John 3:10).

Forgiveness – an essential principle of our faith – is possible only if there is a willingness to recognize transgressions and to submit to the procedures established by law to sanction them. "No-one who conceals transgressions will prosper, but one who confesses and forsakes them will obtain mercy" (Proverbs 28:13).

Forgiveness can only be effective when the wicked "turn from their sin and do what is lawful and right" (Ezekiel 33:14-16). "If we confess our sins, he who is faithful and just will forgive us our sins and cleanse us from all unrighteousness" (1 John 1:9). Nothing can be further from these ideas than the plan for concealment and impunity, and the obvious interests of the Right and the Armed Forces to force this plan through.

No reasons of state or pragmatic considerations can persuade us to turn from the Lord's explicit and unequivocal command: "seek righteousness" (Zephaniah 2:3), because "by justice a king gives stability to the land" (Proverbs 29:4). "And what does the Lord require of you but to do justice?" (Micah 6:8); "Speak out, judge righteously, defend the rights of the poor and needy" (Proverbs 31:9); "but in every nation anyone who fears him and does what is right is acceptable to him" (Acts 10:34-35); "pursue righteousness" (2 Timothy 2:22). In the last analysis "the Lord loves justice" (Psalm 37:28; Proverbs 21:3; Isaiah 61:8).

Without justice, it will never be possible to build a social community marked by peace, harmony and reconciliation: "The violence of the wicked will sweep them away, because they refuse to do what is just" (Proverbs 21:7). Rather, as Christians we feel the actuality of God's call. "Cain, where is your brother Abel....your brother's blood is crying out to me from the ground" (Genesis 4:9-10).

**We call upon:**
- **The people,** to fight suspicion, individualism, consumerism and isolation; to reflect together and in social organizations on the difficult situation our country is traversing; to reject impunity in as many different ways as possible; not to give way to frustration and passivity, but rather to rally to the organizations which love life and which fight for truth and justice.
- **Our brothers in Catholic military chaplaincies and the Uniformed Evangelical Movement (MEU),** to end all forms of complicity (by commission or by ommission) with attempts to close the book on these issues; to join their voices to the cry for justice, bearing in mind that it is essential to "obey God rather than any human authority" (Acts 5:27-29; 4:19-20).
- **The Armed Forces,** to assume their responsibilities and, if they genuinely wish to be reconciled with the people, to respect the institutions, authorities and values of democratic order.
- **The Judiciary,** to apply the law with equal firmness to all

citizens of Chile, whether civilian or military and, in keeping with God's word: "they shall render just decisions for the people. You must not distort justice; you must not show partiality" (Deuteronomy 16:18-19).

- **The Government of Chile,** to fulfil its commitments under the two programmes of Concertation for Democracy, by repealing or revoking Decree Law No 2191 of 1978 concerning amnesty, and seek ways to establish truth and justice; to stop making concessions to people who do not believe in democracy and are simply seeking to protect their own interests; and to trust in the mobilizing power of the people, which in the past has proved fruitful in creating a sound basis for society.

As Christians, we feel that the time has come to put our commitment to God's kingdom to the test and to prove our conviction that "the righteous shall inherit the land" (Psalm 37:29). In view of the gravity of the situation facing our country, we have only two options: for life and justice or for cowardice and impunity.

No half-measures are possible (Revelation 3:15-16).

---

### FASIC rejects "Final Point" law

SANTIAGO, Chile, 8 November 1995 (ALC). The Social Aid Foundation of the Christian Churches (FASIC) vigorously rejected a Senate Constitution, Legislation and Justice Commission agreement to propitiate a Final Point law for cases involving human rights violations committed during the military regime.

"The new initiative falls within a general framework characterized by the absolute denial of the observation of justice," FASIC legal team declared. It went on to say that the new norms would make it impossible to clear up the cases of detention-disappearances or executions which occurred under military rule.

The statement added that one of proposed law's main innovations is that cases involving the forced disappearance of persons would now be handled by Military Courts. This "opens the way for the total and immediate application of amnesty."

The proposed law would facilitate, according to FASIC, the "definitive stay of proceedings of these causes," which constitutes a "regression with regard to current legal norms. Currently judges can legally summon, detain and submit to trial those who are accused of crimes under investigation".

The FASIC statement added that according to current norms, neither the antecedents which judges obtain, nor the identity of those who declare, are secret; evidence is not destroyed and even if the penal responsibility of those involved is extinguished, it is their obligation to exhaust the investigation.

With the recently approved legal initiative, all of these and other prerogatives have been eliminated, said the FASIC team. The issue of a Final Point law for human rights violations committed during the military dictatorship was at the forefront last August when President Frei sent a legal project to Congress which sought to speed up the processes in the courts and gave him the power to name the new armed force and police chiefs.

In Parliament, however, sectors which had previously supported the military government, in particular the opposition and right wing Renovación Nacional, negotiated substantial modifications with the Frei government which led to a virtual "final point" law.

This agreement, according to FASIC, will reap the worst results as it implies "no justice, no certain possibility of truth...". Rather, concluded jurists from the mentioned entity, it is an "imprudent, covered up Final Point law, ethically repugnant for the moral conscience of the country."

On the other hand, consulted political analysis confirmed that this was the price the country had to pay for the imprisoning of Gen. Manuel Contreras, declared guilty of the murder of former foreign minister Orlando Letelier.

According to these views, Pinochet accepted the arrest and imprisonment of his former head of security, under the condition that nothing more was said about human rights cases.

Catholic lay people involved in humanitarian organizations have programmed a day of reflection and liturgical celebration for Nov. 25 in order to express their "ethical anger" about these agreements.

At the same time political parties of the left and human rights organizations publicly expressed rejection of the approved project and even led demonstrations in front of the Parliament building (END).

Latin American and Caribbean
Communication Agency (ALC)

# THE LAW AND BIBLICAL PROPHECY

## *Dagoberto Ramírez F.*

As the basis for this critique of the situation in our country today from the standpoint of Christian ethics, I have chosen the message of the prophets of Israel.  In the age of the prophets Amos and later Isaiah, that is, in the 8th and 7th centuries BC, we find a situation which has many points in common with our own.

## Historical background

The prophet Amos denounced social injustice in an age characterized by a) political stability resulting from a series of alliances with the great centres of power of the time; and b) economic prosperity based on productivity and international trade.  Yet, because of the unequal distribution of wealth, this economic boom itself also caused social disintegration.  Wealth was concentrated in the hands of a few families while small farmers and peasants grew poorer and poorer. Farmers were despoiled of their land, dispossessed or even taken into slavery because of the financial policy of high-interest loans operated by the powerful classes.  This exploitation took place "legally", that is, in the framework of a legal system geared to the dominant political and economic system.  This administration of justice reinforced a system designed to defend the interests of the minority, even though it engendered poverty and injustice for the majority.  Faced with this state of affairs the monarchic state did little or nothing to improve the situation.  All this happened in the 8th and 7th centuries BC; the resemblance with the situation in Chile today can be no more than fortuitous.

## Prophetic condemnation

In this historical background, Isaiah denounces the legal system which permits the accumulation of possessions in the following terms:

*"Ah, you who make iniquitous decrees,*
*who write oppressive statutes,*
*to turn aside the needy from justice*
*and to rob the poor of my people of their right,*
*that widows may be your spoil,*
*and that you may make the orphans your prey!"*

(Isaiah 10:1-2)

Isaiah specifically condemns the social class which legislates – the ones who create such injust laws. This situation engenders poverty and the abuse of power through  formally legalized social injustice.
The prophet says:

> *"Ah, you who join house to house,*
> *who add field to field,*
> *until there is room for no-one but you,*
> *and you are left to live alone*
> *in the midst of the land."*

(Isaiah 5:8)

The prophet condemns the steady enrichment of a minority which leads a life of luxury, of opulence and of wasteful extravagance (Isa. 5:11-17).  There are no legal or ethical limits or boundaries to control this state of affairs.

But they have forgotten two things: first, that the poor who sustain the system by their labour pay the cost of the lifestyle of the minority; and second, that divine justice demands equality of rights and opportunities for the whole people.

They thus lost all sense of justice, of right, and of moral and ethical values which govern the life of society.

Since this situation of injustice is protected by the law, the prophet denounces those who make unjust laws (Isa. 10:1-14) and secondly, those whose task is to administer justice.

Pointing to the legislators the prophet says:

> *"Ah, you who call evil good*
> *and good evil,*
> *who put darkness for light*
> *and light for darkness,*
> *who put bitter for sweet*
> *and sweet for bitter."*

(Isaiah 5:20)

And pointing to the administrators of justice the prophet says:

> *"Ah, you who acquit the guilty for a bribe,*
> *and deprive the innocent of their rights!"*

(Isaiah 5:23)

Those who legislate and those who administer justice go against what is right: they distort the right and allow themselves to be corrupted out of personal or class interests.

## In sum

What does all this have to say for Chile today?

1. The root of all evil is the ambition for economic power, the accumulation of wealth, and the unfair administration of that wealth.

2. This unjust system is also subject to God's judgment. God's justice does not forget or forgive human injustice. For God there is no amnesty. God does not forget, nor does he allow human injustice to be forgotten. No-one will go unpunished.

3. If there is to be genuine justice, it is essential to tackle the root of the evil. This means denouncing dominant economic-political power and its mechanisms and structures of the control of power.

4. The prophets' condemnation sheds light on our present situation. The free-market economic model with its neo-liberal ideology concentrates power in a few hands, produces poverty, and places the majority of the population outside the system. The legal system places the poor outside the law and seeks to stifle their protest. The time has come for us to overturn the legal system and let true justice flourish.

Jesus of Nazareth inspires us in this quest when he says:

*"Blessed are those who hunger and thirst for righteousness, for they will be filled."*

(Matt. 5:6)

It is time those who demand justice were truly heard.

## Questions

What can be done today to answer demands for justice?

We must insist on the importance of education for human rights at all levels. This process was neglected when our country went through the transition from military government to democracy. Human rights were dealt with at a high and formal level. It was not accompanied by a process of education and reflection among the people. The effect has been to "disarm" opinion. Subsequent events have confirmed that the need to insist that impunity is wrong is something which cannot be neglected.

This must take place at the formal as well as informal levels sometimes called popular education, within political or neighbourhood organizations, cultural centres, women's groups and youth.

The essential content of this educational process must both denounce and announce. The two are complementary. Denouncing refers to the past, to what has happened; announcing looks to the present and what lies ahead. The church, civil society, and popular organizations must raise their voices to speak out publicly on the abuses of the past. But their denunciations must be accompanied by a message for the future. That is, what we must avoid, and what we must proclaim: the rights of every individual.

This two-dimensional approach is a way for us as a people to come to terms with our historical consciousness. As we interpret the past we become aware of the present, which in turn enables us to look to the future in newness of life, the new future which we wish to build in our country.

# THE ABSENCE OF JUSTICE

## *Héctor Salazar Ardiles*

Talking about impunity in Chile immediately evokes a tragic chapter in our history. So many images of suffering, violence, arrogance, frustration, hopes and failures inevitably spring to mind.

This is not a problem of the past, however, it is one that is very much present today and which inevitably ties us to that past. Impunity is the main reason why that past cannot be put behind us and continues to affect us so dramatically today.

It would seem to me that first and foremost we need to change our language.

What we will in fact be talking about, more than impunity, is the lack of justice. Perhaps the word impunity indeed fails to convey all the shortcomings of justice in evidence in this country. It addresses only one aspect of that absence of justice to which I have referred: the punishment of criminals.

There is no doubt that the problem runs much deeper than that. The shortcomings go much further than just the failure to sanction offenders. The violators of human rights are simply not imprisoned. There are no measures that affect them. The time has come for us to agree on the language we use: what best encapsulates what we are now experiencing in Chile is *the absence of justice.*

Of course, this phenomenon was most clearly perceived during the military dictatorship. But this absence of justice, unfortunately, is not restricted to that historical period alone. It is also being harshly felt today among the poorest sectors and the youth.

Is this lack of justice deliberate, or is it a consequence of a systemic structure ?

A first attempt at an answer would seem to indicate that at least two factors combine to produce this situation.

In the first place the lack of justice was most glaring under the perversity and wickedness of the dictatorship. It is unprecedented in the history of Chile. Nothing in our history was that cruel.

It suffices to give just one example. In defining the crime of homicide, one assumed that there had to be a corpse. If there was none, a crime could not be established. No thought, however, had ever been given to a case in which the murderer could dispose of the victim's remains. That seemed entirely inconceivable. Whenever in this country's criminal history there was a murderer who tried to hide the victim's corpse, it shocked the entire nation and the case became a focus of attention, receiving extensive press coverage. In such cases, the main thrust of police investigations was to find the mortal remains. When they eventually did, they earned themselves high praise and commendation for a successful investigation.

The criminal was much more strongly condemned by society and by the judicial system, precisely for having tried to hide the corpse. I remember the case of 80 Dardignac Street, dating back to the 1960s, when a flight assistant died during a clandestine abortion and the body was cut up into several pieces to be disposed of. The case occupied an extensive place in our police annals.

Today, this loophole in criminal law has been brought sharply into focus by the cases of forced disappearance of persons. It is impossible under the law to establish that they have been murdered, as no bodies are produced.

This fact explains the present determination to locate the remains of the disappeared.

The repressive crimes committed during the dictatorship were of such magnitude and consequence as to surpass all imaginable limits and therefore explains the profound impact they had on the moral conscience of most Chileans.

It also explains the blunt refusal by the military to accept any responsibilities for such acts. If they did, it would be impossible for the leadership to explain away what happened, let alone justify it.

Consequently, the abyss now dividing the country seems impossible to breach.

The phenomenon is not restricted to our country alone. If we look at the other processes of transition from military dictatorship to democracy in the Southern Cone, we will see that they became possible only to the extent that the violators of human rights were guaranteed increasing degrees of criminal impunity. On those terms the armed forces agreed to return to their barracks.

In the second place, political factors intervened. After wielding absolute power for so long, the armed forces withdrew from government in a position of considerable strength, having shaped an institutional structure that enabled them today to be leading political players. The political coalition that opposed the dictatorship accepted the methods and timetable worked out by the latter as the path of transition to democracy. That was the option supported by most Chileans. Clearly this strategy provided considerable scope for freedom in the country. But it allowed very limited leeway for progress in the domain of justice. Resistance by the military became a stumbling-block in the way of judicial investigations.

Now, we must deal with a situation where the pressure of demands for justice in the wake of the Letelier case is being countered by demands from the military for a halt to further investigations and for the case to be closed once and for all. Military pressure has imposed itself on the government. It, in turn, has been obliged to undertake a legal initiative aimed at finding a "solution" to the problem.

## How can this dilemma be solved ?

For the vast majority in the country – for those active in the domain of human rights, family associations and churches, and political parties opposed to the dictatorship and, in general, those organized sectors that had fought for democracy – the outstanding debt in terms of human rights violations can only be settled by doing justice. For these groups, doing justice means to uncover the truth of what took place, establish the identities of those responsible and subject them to the appropriate sanctions, and all of this within the domain of the courts of justice.

For the Armed Forces and their civilian supporters, the "solution" consists of a clean break with the past, to stop the investigations, to reveal as little as possible and, of course, allowing no sanctions to be applied. This is *lack of justice.*

They are aware that the foregoing is not a "solution". It amounts to the imposition, at any price, of a project that they launched with a *coup d'état* on 11 September 1973. They have stopped at nothing.

An anecdote might serve to clarify whether these initiatives reflect the aspirations of the majority of the people, or whether they conceal formulas for institutionalizing the lack of justice.

The former Secretary-General of the *de facto military* government, Francisco Javier Cuadra, was interviewed on a television programme. Asked whether he had ever lied during his tenure as official government spokesman, he solemnly replied that his conscience was clear and that he had never told a lie in the discharge of his functions. "On the contrary", he said he "had not told the full truth more than once."

This strange concept of truth and untruth, half-truths, or partial truth, is tantamount to lies. If it were only an isolated case it would be unimportant. But this behaviour pattern recurs with growing frequency, making it is extremely difficult to detect the aims of those proposing legislative initiative now making their way through the Congress.

The language used is not clear. Concepts such as truth and reconciliation are used with deliberate ambiguity. It makes for very little transparency.

## So what is really happening?

A political operation apparently has been launched designed to put an end to any further quest for justice. Therefore the need for justice has been and continues to be alive in the nation's moral conscience. It clamours for a solution that is not a product of political engineering, but rather a proposal inspired by ethical and moral values deeply rooted in the national psyche.

No-one denies the existence of objective problems that make it very difficult to obtain justice. But no practical approach can justify renouncing the pursuit of justice for the sake of partial truths.

The only way to rebuild democracy upon solid foundations is never to give up the quest for justice. If it fails to materialize, it will bear the fingerprints of those who impeded it, for posterity to see.

As a matter of priority, the main task will be to forge resolutely ahead with the democratization of the country. Only democracy can make justice possible and defeat impunity.

# BOLIVIA

A little-known but groundbreaking judicial process and trial, which stretched over nine arduous years, finally culminated in 1995 with a guilty verdict against General Luis García Meza. He, fellow members of the Joint Military Command and forty-seven other collaborators were brought up on charges for their role in the 1979 *coup d'état* and for the systematic detention, torture, forced disappearance and killings of political opponents in the months that followed.  García Meza was arrested in 1995 and extradited from Brazil. He is now serving a thirty-years' sentence in the high-security prison of Chonchocorro.  Still, torture continues even under civilian governments, a fact confirmed in recent months by a parliamentary investigative commission[1]. What is perhaps most striking about the impressive public pressure for accountability is the multi-ethnic character of Bolivian society, composed in its great majority of Quechua, Aymara and Tupiguarani peoples. Historically the most exploited social majority, the indigenous population developed resilient and imaginative forms of struggle, in cooperation with a strong labour federation of mining workers and other sectors – ultimately resulting in a form of visible justice. These movements, including representatives of the main Protestant and Catholic churches, are active in the Assembly of Human Rights of Bolivia. The significance of the meticulous work carried out by the organizations of the families of victims, in concert with a national judiciary of great integrity, cannot be underestimated. The following statement was made public some months before the Supreme Court rendered its historic judgement.

# HISTORICAL AND ETHICAL THOUGHTS
## ABOUT THE FOUNDATIONS OF HUMAN RIGHTS

### *Permanent Assembly for Human Rights*

On October 10th, 1992, Bolivia celebrated the 10th anniversary of the end of the military dictatorships and the return to democracy. An assessment of the decade highlighted a series of shortcomings in the functioning of the democratic system, particularly in terms of economic and social measures that now cause a steady deterioration in the population's already low standard of living.

Likewise social and political forces have re-grouped and a very special power structure and style of democratic representativity have been created, marked by "pragmatism" devoid of principles. An agreement was reached between the dictators of the past and long-standing democrats, thereby discrediting the democratic principles for which the people fought during nearly two decades of military dictatorship.

Thus, attempts are being made from within the spheres of political and economic rule to draw a veil of impunity over those who either held power during the dictatorship or benefited from it. Regular objections are raised nonetheless to the appointment of individuals who held high-ranking positions under the dictatorships, to senior posts in the democratic governments. They are reinstated at considerable cost to the people.

While much greater freedom prevails, the effects of totalitarianism and the barbaric styles of the past still haunt the corridors of state security agencies. Former agents of repression remain as trusted police officers and civil servants in the Ministry of Interior.

This subtle legacy of totalitarianism and other more open activities, like the continual failure to respect the independence of state powers, with a view to subordinating the legislature or the judiciary to the executive, endanger democratic institutions. The most significant event was the case brought against former cabinet ministers by political and union leaders, journalists, members of the military, priests and relatives of the victims.

The witnesses brought attention to offences committed under the dictatorship, closely linked to drug trafficking, to the harassment, torture, and assassinations of Marcelo Quiroga Santa Cruz, the Socialist Party leader, Carlos Flores and Roberto Vega, senior leaders of the MIR[2], and to economic crimes and unlawful personal gains.

The state prosecutor and the group that brought the case against García Meza and his colleagues – made up of the Bolivian Workers' Confederation, the Bolivian Assembly for Human Rights, the Bolivian Press Workers' Federation, the University of Bolivia and the Association of Relatives of the Detainees, Missing Persons and Martyrs for National Liberation, *inter alia* – presented the court with 2000 authenticated legal documents as clear-cut evidence against the dictatorship.

The paramilitary involved in the assassination of leaders and systematic repression of the Bolivian people were identified. In terms of economic offences, it was proven that García Meza and his colleagues misappropriated over 235 million dollars belonging to the Bolivian state.

For the first time in the legal history of the country, the Supreme Court of Justice presided over the reconstruction of a criminal offence: the killing of eight MIR leaders by paramilitary forces under the command of the Minister of the Interior at the time, Luis Arce Gomez.

The evidence was so strong that it could not be refuted by the witnesses for the defence or the documents submitted by García Meza and the accused. In fact, the only documentary evidence they could produce were certificates of good conduct which even they did not believe.

In October, 1990, the trial was suddenly brought to a halt by a suit filed against eight ministers of the Supreme Court for prevarication. This triggered a conflict of powers that shook the very institutional foundations of democracy.

After being reinstated, the highest legal court closed the probatory phase; eight years had elapsed since the beginning of the proceedings, the only case brought against an ex-dictator in Latin America to date. One hundred and nine 200-page documents had been submitted, making up a total of 21,000 sheets, the largest file in Bolivian legal history.

The committee that brought the case against García Meza and the lawyers for the prosecution requested the Supreme Court to sentence the accused (1994) because on December 20th, six members of the supreme court, familiar with the entire proceedings, will have fulfilled their statutory term of 10 years; if the court failed to make a ruling, there was a danger of a lengthy delay as the new members of the court as of January 1993 would have to make a detailed review of the file. This would take an indefinite amount of time.

The "political trial of the century" entered, in 1995, its final phase; the arguments put forward by the defence are being heard, after which the Supreme Court of Justice has two weeks to hand down its final ruling. Although proceedings have been anything but smooth, there is every reason to maintain that the provisions of the anachronistic Bolivian legal system have been fulfilled.

While the Supreme Court has now done its duty, within the purview of the law, the exemplary firmness of the prosecution, which had to overcome endless difficulties, deserves special mention. The prosecution is not asking to avenge the dead and missing. However, he does indeed seek justice to establish a precedent to ensure that the tragic events under the dictatorship that took power in the country in July 1980 should never again occur.

The people await the final sentence in the firm belief it is not an individual that is being judged, but a criminal system that has flourished on many occasions. The trial is a condemnation of dictatorial, anti-democratic methods and marks renewed respect for the established order and human rights. The lessons drawn from this trial will be held up as an example of what must never happen again; they will have to be taken into consideration by those in power, mindful, henceforth, of the fact that there can be no impunity. Those who trample the laws and commit offences will be liable to sanctions.

Those who fell for the noble ideals of justice and liberty must not be betrayed. Their cause is common to one and all.

### The victims

Many mothers, wives, children and relatives endured the forced disappearance of their loved ones during the dictatorial regimes that governed Bolivia for nearly two decades. The Association of Relatives of the Detainees, Missing Persons and Martyrs for National Liberation (ASOFAMD) is the entity that represents the victims of such crimes against humanity.

Immediately after the reinstatement of democratic freedoms in 1982, the government of Dr. Hernán Siles Suazo created a Committee to Investigate Forced Disappearances by means of a supreme decree. It supplied the requisite facilities and guarantees to begin investigations, particularly into the dictatorship that had just been brought to a close.

Work by this committee, with the active participation of ASOFAMD, shed light on a series of events that had remained in the shadows of the dictatorships until now. The basements used as cells in the Ministry of the Interior were discovered; messages etched by prisoners were identified; clandestine cemeteries were found; bodies were exhumed and major testimonies were obtained from agents and paramilitary staff involved in the assassinations and disappearances.

As a result of the tenacious work of ASOFAMD, which is part of the Latin American Federation of Families of Missing Persons (FEDEFAM), the National Congress declared forced disappearance a crime against humanity, that is, the worst offence that can be committed against a person and society. It thus reiterated the declarations of the Organization of American States and Venezuela – the only country at that time to have adopted such a resolution.

The information gathered by ASOFAMD made it possible to establish that 166 detainees disappeared in Bolivia under dictatorial regimes: 76 under Gen. Hugo Banzer Suarez, 34 under Gen. Alfredo Ovando Candia, 24 under the brief reign of Col. Alberto Natush Busch, 4 under Gen. René Barrientos Ortuno and 28 under the last dictatorship, that of Gen. Luis García Meza Tejada.

These latter cases were described in full detail when evidence was being submitted in the trial against García Meza and his colleagues by the FEDEFAM Secretary of International Relations, Loyola Buzman, who gave the country's Supreme Court written accounts of tortured, missing and assassinated citizens as of the military coup in July, 1980, and throughout the *de facto* regime.

An investigatory committee of family members of the victims pieced together the criminal events, presented details concerning the places and times of detention, assassinations and disappearances.

According to this committee, 28 people disappeared during the dictatorial regime of García Meza and 52 assassinations took place, above all those of Marcelo Quiroga Santa Cruz, the socialist leader, Gualberto Vega Yapura, Carlos Flores Bedregal during the assault on the Bolivian Workers' Confederation, and the subsequent Harrington Street massacre, when eight leaders of the then clandestine MIR were killed, in addition to other workers, peasants and students.

There are hundreds of other victims of the dictatorships, who were imprisoned, tortured and exiled, yet have received no form of protection under the democratic system. The wives, children and relatives of the missing and killed are left to their own devices; they have no legal channels to claim moral or material compensation, physical or psychological care, not to mention rehabilitation programmes that do not even exist.

In this respect, the democratic regime has been left with the sequels of the dictatorships in the form of hundreds of direct or indirect victims, who suffered the outrages of totalitarianism.

## Identification and prosecution of persons who violated human rights

At the beginning of 1984, political parties, trade unions, families of detainees and missing persons together with human rights institutions began proceedings before the National Congress against the former dictator, Luis García Meza, and many of his colleagues for violations of the constitution, armed uprising, organization of illegal groups, violations of freedom of the press, assassinations, human rights violations and economic damage to the state.

Two years later, on February 25, 1986, the national Parliament referred the accusations to the Supreme Court by a two-thirds majority. On March 15 of this same year, the defendants thus charged were brought before the country's highest court of justice to be judged according to the provisions of article 127 of the Political Constitution of the state and the laws of 31 October 1884 and 23 October 1944.

On April 7, the former dictator, Luis García Meza, appeared in court to answer the charges brought against him. Police and military protection was so heavy in Sucre that the city was virtually under siege. The phase of confessions by the accused, which lasted three years and three months, had thus begun.

As expected, the former dictator and his colleagues denied all the charges; while they attempted to abide by normal democratic legal practices, in the end, several fled. The first to disappear in early 1989 was García Meza, who absconded and was subsequently held in contempt of court and judged *in absentia.*

Six months later, the Supreme Court began the hearings. This was one of the most important phases in this historic trial. The highest legal court received evidence from the prosecution, comprising testimonies from over 50 witnesses, starting with the overthrown constitutional president, Lidia Gueller Tejada.

A series of major documentary proof and heart-rending testimonies revealed the magnitude of administrative impunity and violence under the dictatorial regime, stirring the historic memory of the people. Above all, however, the case against the former dictator was experienced as an irrefutable demand for justice.

People are waiting for a final ruling that embodies nation-wide rejection of dictatorial, anti-democratic methods and the desire to respect the law and human rights. For the country, this means renewed trust in justice and a well-deserved national tribute to those who fell victim to impunity, defending noble ideals of justice and liberty.

There is still a latent mistrust of a rule of law that has only too often given way to the economic and political power of dictators or the imperialistic leanings of world powers.

A blatant example of just this is the arrest and extradition to the United States for trial of former Col. Luis Arce Gomez, the feared Minister of the Interior under the García Meza dictatorship, discrediting Bolivian justice and underestimating efforts to establish precedents against dictatorial impunity. This is further compounded by the fact that the fate of the case against the dictatorship does not appear to be one of the current government's main concerns as García Meza and at least four other accused parties have fled and gone underground, and have so far not been captured and detained.

The government, as representative of the democratic state, has not moved beyond declarations of its intention to detain the key person accused. García Meza remains free, his protectors and accomplices enjoy complete impunity and any efforts or demands to enforce the law appear insufficient.

Many victims of the dictatorships are awaiting moral compensation for the atrocities they endured as a result of the totalitarianism that ruled the country for so many years. But the entire country is waiting for the state to shoulder its responsibilities and take immediate action, both through the executive, which must arrest the fugitives, and the judiciary, which must hand down a sentence.

## Legal standards, relevant legislation and administrative measures

With the exception of proceedings against state dignitaries, which are referred to the supreme court, the Bolivian legal system provides that criminal cases shall be tried by the ordinary courts. Likewise, in the case of common law or private offences, the Penal Code defines the sanctions for each offence, subject to the principles of the political constitution of the country.

Insofar as the Bolivian legal system is concerned, principles like the statute of limitations, retroactivity, fair trial or amnesty are rooted in the universal principle of respect for human rights. Strange as it may seem, they also protect parties put on trial for the violation of these rights. The statute of limitations, which defines the time during which penal action may be taken, depends on the type of offence. There is no special rule for offences committed under totalitarian regimes. Similarly, retroactivity, which is designed to ensure the accused party or the criminal is given the lightest, or most favourable, sentence also applies to infringements of human rights.

In general, the right to a fair trial is recognised; both the accused and the prosecution are given the same opportunity to appear at all stages of the trial. Above all, the right of defence is guaranteed. However, this principle has been undermined several times, not specifically in proceedings against parties who committed offences under authoritarian regimes but within the framework of democratic systems. The right to a fair trial is further guaranteed by the Bolivian legal system as the constitution forbids the creation of arbitrary or special courts, whatever the circumstances.

Likewise, sentences are expressly provided for by law; only sanctions defined prior to a given offence may be applied.

The President of the Republic or the National Senate is empowered to pardon common criminals; in the event of high treason or assassination, however, a maximum sentence of 30 years imprisonment has been established, with no right to clemency.

According to the constitution and in light of the type of offence committed, the jurisdiction or competent court for the trial may not be chosen unilaterally or arbitrarily. Military courts are recognized *de facto*, but for offences specific to a military career. Special courts cannot be set up for any given kind of offence.

Proceedings against the former dictator, Luis García Meza, sparked a lengthy debate, as a result of which subordinates were brought to court instead of just ministers of state, as should have been the case. Even paramilitary staff was thus judged in the supreme court, holding up the course of justice as the defendants used various legal tricks. Finally, the political constitution of the state provides that no one shall take orders to commit acts contrary to the constitution; the principle of due obedience is therefore not recognised as mitigating circumstances in the case of offences carried out on "orders from above" under authoritarian regimes that violate human rights.

Democracy has called into question a number of aspects of the legal system and has, in particular, highlighted corruption and delays in justice. This situation has led to the creation of the National Council to Reform and Modernize the Judiciary, which has up to the end of 1994 to publish its report.

While the political constitution of the state and the codes have not yet been amended, there is a trend towards the adoption of reforms to modernize the administration of justice. Most legislators agree on the need to reform the political constitution of the state. This will broaden people's participation in the democratic system and improve state mechanisms so as to better  defend the rights enshrined in the constitution itself.  In turn, this will preserve the tenets of economic and social policy that refer, for example, to the state's duty to protect workers and to provide health care and education.

# NOTES

1.  This parliamentary report is entitled *Denuncia de Torturas A Ciudadanos Sindicados de Alzamiento Armado* (Resolución Camaral no. 68 de Abril de 1994). See also an informative summary of a speech given by Yves Mignot (ACAT, France), entitled *Le Destin de l'Impunité en Amérique latine: le cas particulier de Bolivie,* delivered in February 1996 in Madrid, Spain, at a seminar on impunity in Latin America -y ed.

2.  Movimento de la Izguierda Revolucionària - Left Revolutionary Movement.

# EL SALVADOR

El Salvador, Central America's most populous country, has endured some of the most brutal, gross and systematic violations yet seen in the hemisphere. In twelve years of civil war, from 1980 through to 1991, church-based and other human rights organizations have documented the deaths or disappearance of tens of thousands of persons. The fifty-year history, beginning in the 1930s, of organized attempts by workers and peasants to escape poverty by obtaining better wages and decent living conditions met with continuous official repression and violence. In late 1979 war broke out between popular armed insurgency movements and the Army in which civilian populations were bombed and massacred. The 1980 murder of Roman Catholic Archbishop Oscar Romero, and killings of many other church religious and clergy during that period became powerful symbols of the cruelty of the regime and gave impetus finally to calls for peace negotiations. A Peace Agreement was signed in 1991 between the Salvadorean Government and the FMLN (Farabundo Marti Front for National Liberation). This accord provided for a Commission of the Truth to render a remarkable account of the flagrant human rights violations which occurred in that country. Entitled "From Madness to Hope: the 12-Year War in El Salvador", the voluminous report details with candor and chronological precision the cases and patterns of violence perpetrated by the military and the security forces upon the civilian population. The publication of that UN report was a landmark event for El Salvador and the entire region.

# THEOLOGICAL REFLECTIONS ON THE REPORT
# OF THE TRUTH COMMISSION

### *Jon Sobrino*

## Summary

The Report of the Truth Commission is an exceptional document of fundamental importance for the new El Salvador. Its contents express the evil in the country and its dynamic, but the very fact of its being published is good news and a blessing, and displays the powerful tradition of truth existing in the country. In view of the' reactions to it – such as the amnesty – which seek to cheat a whole people, it is essential to create hope for the country.

The Report of the Truth Commission can be analysed from various angles, including the theological one. In comparison with other analyses this may offer only a few minimum basic elements, but these may also be of special value in the present situation, for two reasons. The first is that realities such as grace and sin, truth and hope, can shape politics, society, the economy and the law and help them to avoid being corrupted. The second is that these theological truths can also provide society with utopian horizons, without which it cannot survive with a minimum of humanity.

It is from this perspective that the present analysis of the Report of the Truth Commission has been prepared.

## 1. A moment of grace: the impossible has become possible

*First proposition: The Report, even with its limitations, is the most important official document in the country's recent history. It has become a symbol of truth, subversion and liberation. It must be a foundational document for a new El Salvador. From a Christian perspective it is good news, and a moment of grace.*

The publication of this Report has had an unprecedented impact in a country where people are no longer surprised by anything. We need to examine why that is so.

The Report confirms what people were already saying, and experts on human rights already knew. It has certain limitations, some obvious and acknowledged by the writers themselves, due to the short deadline given to collect and analyse such a quantity of facts. The Report does not recount all the violations of human rights committed in this country; that was not its purpose. It seeks only to illustrate with significant examples the patterns of criminal behaviour in the eighties.

There are also other limitations of a qualitative nature. There is self-censorship, either for lack of absolute certainty about the facts in some cases, or for understandable political reasons when it came to mentioning the names of civilian members of the oligarchy, death squads, successive governments and the judiciary, the U.S. embassy and various U.S. government agencies. The failure to define the responsibilities of the FMLN [Frente Farabundo Martí de Liberación National – Farabundo Martí National Liberation Front] in each of its groups is a further limitation. Human rights experts would also have liked to see the Report make more headway in the technical investigation of certain cases, rather than simply compiling and collating existing information about them. The Report is not perfect, but its impact remains unprecedented.

In fact, the Report itself was unprecedented in modern times. It was prepared by a prestigious and internationally representative group of authors and appeared at a propitious moment, when the international community, including the new government of the USA, received it and its recommendations. The real underlying reasons for its impact lie deeper, however, and this brings us to its significance.

I begin with two very brief reflections of a philosophical nature, which may help us to understand the Report's radical significance. It is a known anthropological fact that we human beings develop knowledge when we express it in words. In "saying what something is" we come "know" what we already perceive intellectually. Verbal expression is part of the structure of knowledge. Something like this has taken place with the Report. When it collects, systematizes, analyses and interprets data it is saying what we already knew, but putting it all into words and publishing it helps us to know it better. Moreover, as the facts set out in the Report touch very directly the ethical dimension of human life, we are all existentially involved. We cannot avoid facts which are aired publicly.

A well-known metaphysical tenet is that truth seeks expression. This is what happened in the Report. After many years of official silence, "the Salvadorean truth has made itself heard". It describes an objective reality which goes beyond the personal aims and intentions of its authors. The reality of oppression has finally succeeded in truly making itself heard and in demanding to be corrected. The report has become almost a sacramental symbol of our truth.

It is not commonplace truth that has made itself heard in the Report, but the truth of age-old concealed oppression. The Report concludes that almost all the leading officials "have lied". Attempts to lay all responsibility for crimes at the door of the FMLN, while praising the Armed Forces as defenders of the good, has been shown to be a lie.

The authors of this lie are many. They include successive Presidents (the ruling Junta, Magaña, Duarte, Cristiani), the Ministers of Defence (García, Vides Casanova, Larios, Ponce), the various Presidents of the Supreme Court, newspapers such as *El Diario de Hoy*, the U.S. ambassadors (Hinton, Pickering, Corr, Walker) and Presidents (Reagan and Bush). All of them knew the truth but remained silent and/or covered up crimes. As we now see in published form, they all lied brazenly.

The Report does not ignore the FMLN, but it is held accountable for only 5% of the recorded violations. It clears the FMLN of all charges of torture or massacres, practices common to the Armed Forces. Monsignor Romero, Monsignor Rivera, Father Ellacuría, human rights institutions (among others the Archbishop's Tutela Legal – Legal Trust – which was severely attacked by the military and the U.S. embassy), the Committees of Mothers of the disappeared and political detainees, and the peasants who testified to repression even at the risk of greater repression: all of them told the truth.

The Report has not only told the truth. It has unmasked the massive and sustained official lie. It shows that Salvadorean society has in effect been the opposite of the official picture. The Report explodes the myth of official language, its lies.[1] It is not only beneficial but also liberating, a genuine victory of the truth over falsehood. This explains its great impact and the reactions it has provoked.

The Report has become an obligatory point of reference in the history of our country, a document on which, we hope, a new El Salvador can be founded. Of course it does not have the legal weight of a Constitution nor the programmatic value of the Chapultepec Agreements which ought to guide us into the immediate future. But it does have great potential – even more than that of the Constitution – to overcome the past and point the way into the future through telling the truth. Lawyers and legislators would do well to keep it before them when they interpret, apply or reform the Constitution.

Thus the Report is a historic document, less because it is "unique", or "unrepeatable" than because it creates history. Reactions to it are forceful both in favour and against. The latter are the more powerful. They have means and they use them to discredit or ignore the Report, and kill it through a thousand debates, interpretations and delays in implementation. They wish to deprive the Report of its capacity to create history. So the Report must be known – read – and recognized as something which belongs essentially to our history; if we do not know it, we do not know ourselves. We hear people saying these days, "No-one should graduate from senior school or university without having read the Report". How true! "The Report must be read in the family" as the Bible once was.

The Report has become so important because it symbolises the truth and the need to break with the past. It therefore carries double weight – it has the weight of the text and the weight of the symbol. As a text, it speaks to readers and moves them, and as a symbol it moves human beings and society as a whole.

In theological terms, we might say that the Report is good news for the poor. Not for the horrors it recounts, but because it puts the real situation into words which challenges the age-old lying of the oppressors. Truth is always good news for the poor. The Report is also good news, or at least the beginning of good news for the poor because of its recommendations. If these are implemented, many things will change in this country, especially for the poor.

This good news is also grace. It is a gift, something unexpected and miraculous. "The impossible has come to pass". Given the history of duplicity in this country, it is a miracle that the Report was published.

The Report is "costly" grace, not the "cheap" grace, against which Bonhoeffer protested. It tells of the unbelievable suffering of the people and of the countless martyrs. They have made it possible. The Salvadorean people have more than earned this Report.

The words of the Magnificat express what hope there is for the poor in the Report:

*"He has shown strength with his arm; he has scattered the proud in the thoughts of their hearts, he has brought down the powerful from their thrones, and lifted up the lowly; he has filled the hungry with good things, and sent the rich away empty"* (Luke 1:51-53).

## 2. Structural sin: a crucified people

*Second proposition: The Report exposes both death and its concealment, a dynamic of evil which shocks people here and abroad.*

Reading the Report, one is filled with horror. It is not easy to keep going to the end. It displays what the ancients called the *mysterium iniquitatis*. One can only shudder. But it also produces indignation at the lack of punishment, the impunity, with which these things were committed and concealed by the country's authorities.

### *The violence done to life*

The New Testament says that "the love of money is the root of all kinds of evil" (1 Timothy 6:10). This creed begets violence and deceit. The Report makes this clear.

It all really starts with the seventh commandment, "You shall not steal". In El Salvador, the evils of the present began a century ago with the plundering of the people's land, its means of subsistence. To keep this plunder and increase it, the oligarchy set the armed forces, security services, paramilitaries and death squads to work for them, in violation of the fifth commandment, "You shall not murder". They then concealed the truth in violation of the eighth commandment, "You shall not bear false witness ...".

Scandal and cover-up are interrelated. When there is scandal, cover-up follows. The bigger the concealment, the greater the scandal. We refer to the cover-up as violating the eighth commandment because it is the most usual and most serious form of social lying. Most usual, because the media continually and regularly contribute to covering things up, as *El Diario de Hoy* does, through the statements of the authorities, the Armed Forces, the judiciary, and the U.S. embassy. Most serious, because what is concealed is the slow death by poverty, endured by the majority, and the swift and violent death suffered by those who seek to escape from poverty.

This cover-up does violence to the truth and  promotes impunity both for crimes already committed and for future crimes (because continuing to commit them is made easy).

The second commandment – "You shall not make wrongful use of the name of the Lord your God" – is taken seriously in our part of the world. Still, official speeches here tend to be obfuscating in the extreme, and usually end by invoking God's blessing. Salvadorean presidents usually end their speeches with "God bless you". The blessing Salvadoreans want is for the presidents to speak the truth and not cover things up. Very recently, the Minister of Defence – who is mentioned often in the Report – ended his appearance on television with "God bless you". During his talk he attacked the Report instead of humbly asking forgiveness. The President of the Supreme Court has said, "God alone can remove me from office". In this way he becomes not only an accomplice in cover-ups but a perverter of religion.

The seventh commandment says, "You shall have no other gods before me. You shall not make for yourself an idol ..." (Deuteronomy 5,7f.). Jesus said, in the same vein,  "No one can serve two masters; for a slave will... hate the one and love the other,..... You cannot serve God and wealth" (Matthew 6:24). Accumulating wealth to the extent of plundering is in violation of  both the seventh and the first commandment of God's law.[2]

The Report does not settle for a structural theoretical explanation of the origin of violence but notes that there are "patterns of criminal behaviour", "systematically organized atrocities", "generic, institutionalized impunity". But the scale and frequency of the violations show that there are structural roots which produce not only forms of individual behaviour but also institutional behaviour. The economic oligarchy and the military in our country have clearly been structurally violent.

### *The violence done to truth*

Violation of the truth has taken place on a massive scale, institutionally and with structural inevitability, through official discourse and through the media. The Report shows that government officials not only failed to investigate earlier reports by responsible human rights bodies, but that the Executive, the Armed Forces, the judiciary and the US embassy all frequently covered up the truth and openly lied to the public. The Minister of Defence, for example, publicly denied for three years that he and the High Command had anything to do with the murders of the six Jesuit priests and their two housekeepers at the University.

The government have vigorously attacked anyone who disagreed with the official version of the facts. They not only diverted attention from the facts, or lied about them, but also misrepresented them in such a way that the victims (peasants, members of popular movements and Christian movements or of the FMLN) were presented as the culprits. Targets of terrorism – printing-houses, radios, trade union premises, churches, human rights institutions, victims like Monsignor Romero, Herbert Anaya, and Father Ellacuría – were represented as instigators of terrorism. Thus the recommendation of the Report to restore the honour of the victims is entirely justified. But it will be difficult to put into practice because for officials to restore honour to the victims would be tantamount to self-indictment.

This disgraceful combination of neglect, concealment, cover-ups and distortion made possible the horror described in the Report. It also explains why the judiciary took no action, out of conflict of interest or fear of official reprisals. The overall result of this dynamic of evil is what Monsignor Romero came to describe as "the empire from hell".

### *A report for everyone, where all must read about themselves*

Everyone, not only Salvadoreans but especially people in the First World, should read the Report, or another one like it – say, from Guatemala or Haiti (when they are published). In the face of such aberrations in the human family, produced by members of the human family, we should all ask ourselves about our responsibility by omission or commission in these matters. Not only those Salvadoreans who are mentioned in the Report, but those whose names do not appear – the oligarchy, the media, professional bodies, universities, trade unions, members of religious orders, colleges and churches, must question themselves closely.[3]

The question must also be asked outside El Salvador. There was clear and direct foreign involvement in these events. The countries of the North cannot simply rejoice now that the truth is being told, and leave the blame to the Salvadoreans alone, as if geopolitical considerations and their own economic and military policies had nothing to do with it, not to mention the lucrative business of arms sales. Only thus can the First World come to see itself as it truly is, beyond political discussions on democracy or failed socialism or the new Europe, philosophical discussions on modernity and post-modernity, and ecclesiastical discussions for or against the new Catechism. Father Ellacuría said, "The First World will see itself as in an inverted mirror when it looks at what it produces in the Third World". This Report offers a very special mirror.

This is particularly important to the U.S.A. Successive U.S. administrations have been responsible for much that is related in the Report. Financial aid to the Salvadorean government (the famous "million dollars a day"), diplomatic aid (pressure on Latin American and European governments) and military aid (training of elite battalions in the United States, such as the Atlacatl which was responsible for the massacre of El Mozote and the UCA murders, and military advisers in the country) have been directly or indirectly responsible for the atrocities related in the Report.

The Reagan and Bush governments were responsible for the shameful cover-up of the truth. This encouraged cover-ups and lying here. The logic was, "If they who are democrats par excellence tell lies, why shouldn't we?" In this connection, the official U.S. reactions to some of the crimes related in the Report are revealing.

On 2 December 1980 four North American missionaries were murdered. Secretary of State Alexander Haig, on 18 March 1981, told the House Foreign Affairs Committee: "It seems that the vehicle in which the missionaries were being driven may have accidentally jumped a stop".

On 10 December 1981, the Atlacatl battalion carried out the El Mozote massacre in which, according to the Report, hundreds of people were "systematically and deliberately executed". The massacre was reported by the *New York Times* and the *Washington Post* of 27 January 1982. On 8 February, Thomas Enders, Assistant Secretary of State for Latin American Affairs, said before the Congress's Committee on Foreign Affairs that although there was evidence of a military confrontation between government forces and the guerrillas, "no evidence can be found to confirm that the government forces had systematically massacred the civilian population", and Elliot Abrams, Assistant Secretary for Human Rights, told the same committee that it was an incident of which the least one can say is that the "guerrillas" were apparently responsible.

On 16 November 1989 the Atlacatl battalion murdered six Jesuits and two employees of the Universidad Centroamericana. The U.S. ambassador, in a press conference, later said, "We are in a war. This is combat and death ... I think President Cristiani is besieged on all sides... I think some things are happening which he would prefer not to happen".

These few examples show how deceitful high officials have been. Now, with the Report's revelations, and under a new democratic government, some people are recognizing their government's serious responsibility in the past. U.S Congressman R.G. Toricelli spoke to this effect on 16 March last before a Congress sub-committee:

> *"As a member of Congress I cannot but be concerned by the involvement of the United States in these tragic events. While some of the most serious violations of human rights were taking place, the Reagan government was giving assurances that in El Salvador progress was being made as to human rights, and was providing substantial financial aid to those very forces identified by the Commission on Truth as those chiefly responsible for the 'great majority of the abuses'."*

We now know what many of us already suspected at the time. Those assurances had no credibility. Instead of using them as had been planned, that is, to exert pressure on the government of El Salvador, the Reagan government used them to stop that pressure, denying that the abuses were continuing. Congress gave the government the means to prevent and oppose those abuses, but, tragically, the Reagan government preferred to see everything through the prism of the anti-communist cause, and thus was able to legitimize these abuses.

## 3. Structural grace: the truth tradition

*Third proposition: El Salvador has a history of speaking out for the truth. It is that tradition that has made the Report of the Commission on Truth possible. The people of El Salvador are the true authors of the Report.*

The content of the Report is a revelation of grave sin, but the fact that it has been written and published is good and positive. The work of the three Commissioners and their team has been important. However, they are not the chief authors of the Report. The chief author is the Salvadorean people.

## *The roots of the tradition of speaking the truth*

The people of El Salvador were convinced that truth and condemnation of abuses, although risky and highly conflictive in the short term, are good things, and bear fruit in the long term. So the cries of death, far from lapsing into silence, have been taken up and made public. That has cost much blood, but it has yielded a great benefit, creating a tradition of speaking out for the truth which has continued up to the present. The Salvadorean people, educated – notably by Monsignor Romero – to speak, have spoken and they are upholding what they have been saying.

In El Salvador we have had cycles of prophetic denunciation since the seventies. I shall illustrate this by focusing on some martyred priests. The first was the cycle of Rutilio Grande, who took up the legacy of speaking out for the truth inherited from Monsignor Luis Chávez and exercised it powerfully. As early as 1970 he publicly and solemnly condemned injustice in the country in his sermon of 6 August. His outspoken demands for the truth reached a peak in his Apopa sermon on 17 February 1977. The second was the cycle of Monsignor Romero, the most illustrious and best known, which requires no comment. The third was the cycle of Father Ellacuría, through his writings and above all his presence on television. His murder in 1989, together with that of so many others, in no way put an end to the tradition of speaking out for the truth – it reinforced it.

I have used the names of martyr priests, because their murder is common knowledge; but also because in a religious country they are the best-known and most outstanding symbols of a much wider tradition. Many others deserve mention: human rights bodies and their spokespersons, María Julia Hernández among the living, Marianella García and Herbert Anaya among the martyrs, national and foreign journalists, the publications of UCA and of the National University, demonstrations by the people's organizations, base communities, trade unions. The relatives, mothers, wives, daughters and sisters of prisoners and the disappeared were the first to go out onto the streets with their message in the most dangerous years of the eighties. Most important were the victims themselves: "The blood that has been shed cries out unceasingly to God", said Monsignor Romero. Monsignor Romero in particular, but also others, provided the "voice of those without a voice". He let the people be heard, taught and inspired them to make themselves heard. "The word endures", he used to say, and that has been fulfilled.

This host of persons and institutions and the struggles of the people's movements and clergy have enabled the truth to be told. They have compelled the authorities to tell the truth, although they do so reluctantly or unwillingly, when they have no other way out.

Why this persistence in speaking out and in telling the truth? One cannot be Salvadorean and Christian without in some way being prophetic. But also out of compassion and love for the victims. That truth, when it comes to be known, is intrinsically capable of moving people to mercy and solidarity. Truth also points *sub specie contrarii* the direction that has to be taken by a just society in which they can live. The truth gives them back dignity and honour. The tradition of truth in El Salvador is one of integrity and compassion. To tell the truth is therefore an important way of expressing love for people. Telling the truth, not forgetting it, is absolutely essential for the building of a new country.

### *The positive currents of history*

The known – and the thousands of unknown – martyrs whose names now appear in an appendix to the Report, have carved out an almost physical track in Salvadorean history, into which we can step and walk "more easily" and tell the truth. In the last few months many peasants have travelled many miles to the Truth Commission to condemn the outrages they have suffered. The truth tradition is only one example. The people of El Salvador have created others in these last few years: the tradition of compassion, of struggle for justice, of celebration, martyrdom and solidarity.

Not all Salvadoreans are actively involved. ARENA (the National Republican Alliance) still wins the elections. But where many have died a death like Jesus' death, defending the victims, and where there are deaths which cry out, if there are a people who take up this cry and resolve to continue Jesus' work, resurrection comes.

### 4. A people cheated?

*Fourth proposition: The old powers still seek to invalidate the truth set out in the Report, and to avoid carrying out its recommendations. They are promoting a culture of "forgetfulness" that knows no responsibility, and creating a culture of "inevitability".*

### *Irresponsibility and the culture of forgetting*

After the Report was published, the official line tried to make people forget not only the reality of the past but also the Report and especially its recommendations. They hope to draw a veil over the past with as little damage as possible.They do so with customary arrogance, using aggressive tactics. Instead of using the Report to heal, they distort it with the slogan "forgive and forget". The forgetting is certainly clear. They do not ask for forgiveness.

They say the Report is unconstitutional, harmful to national reconciliation, intended to wipe out the Armed Forces, a threat to national sovereignty and interventionist. The President of the Supreme Court says it all: "Setting up the Truth Commission was not only a mistake, it was a stupid thing to do".

But the most effective and dangerous attack on the Report has come from President Cristiani, because he seeks to minimize it not with a display of aggressiveness like the others, but with apparent dignity and political good sense.[4] He cannot ignore or discredit it as they do, but he does want to deny that it has any truth that might effectively transform society. Still, he called for an amnesty for all those who might be mentioned in it even before the Report became known – an amnesty shamefully approved by a simple majority in the Assembly and which, to make matters worse, does not apply equally to everyone. Those responsible for murdering the U.S. advisors, members of the FMLN, will not benefit from it.

According to President Cristiani, this amnesty will benefit the country in the spirit of Christian forgiveness. But he has not attempted to show how this amnesty is related to genuine forgiveness. His amnesty devalues the social benefits offered by the Report.

Remembering in order to take vengeance and storing up bitterness benefits no one. But to forget what happened, above all when the causes have not been effectively removed, is a grave social evil. Monsignor Rivera said, "So many wounds cannot be cured by overlooking them. On the contrary, I believe these sores must be uncovered no matter how noxious they are. Then they can be carefully cleansed so that they heal properly and do not become infected again." The Secretary-General of the U.N., Boutros Boutros-Ghali said, "The Scriptures say that 'the truth will make us free'. Salvadoreans will only be able to leave the past behind them once the truth about the past has come to light".

The problem is not forgetting the past but breaking with it. From a  historical point of view the amnesty is therefore harmful.

Amnesty is also harmful from the anthropological and  the social points of view. This country certainly needs reconciliation but the genuinely humanizing element in reconciliation will not be found in quashing or reducing just punishment but in offering and accepting mutual forgiveness. That may well be a consequence of forgiveness but it is not directly humanizing for society. Therefore to put an easy escape from possible punishment before forgiveness and acceptance is not a social good but a serious social evil.

Nor is amnesty good from the Christian perspective, though the President appeals to Christianity so that the amnesty will be well received. In Christian terms forgiveness is granted with generosity, but it happens after the confession of sin. Christians believe that confession is a good thing, not only or principally because it is an exacting exercise, nor even to make amends, but for the liberation it offers and the release from being at odds with oneself. But in this country, as far as we know, no members of the Establishment have asked for forgiveness, nor have they let themselves be forgiven as the FMLN, by contrast, has done.

Amnesty was designed to placate the military, "the perpetually pardoned" as Mario Benedetti says. To give a first example from the U.S.A., Lt. Calley, the man responsible for the My Lai massacre in Vietnam (1968), actually served only four months of a life sentence. In Latin America examples abound in Chile, Uruguay, Brazil. It is important to stress who "the perpetually pardoned" are, because it shows that the problem is in effect structural. "The perpetually pardoned" once again come out winners.

Amnesty is a lost opportunity for reconciliation as a positive act of mutual forgiveness. Amnesty says "nothing will be done" to those responsible for murders. The dynamic of acceptance and forgiveness has been lost. Amnesty makes the profoundly human act of asking and granting forgiveness impossible, makes it commonplace and trivializes it.

Amnesty allows those responsible for atrocities to shut themselves off from their own human future. The theologian Karl Rahner says "only the forgiven know they are sinners". It is difficult to accept forgiveness because it means recognizing oneself as a sinner, but it is also beneficial, because it allows the offended person to open up the future to the sinner and not close it off.

To halt the spiral of antagonism we have to act in ways that will reverse the dynamic of lying. Forgiveness offered and accepted breaks the dynamic of antagonism, division and hatred. Amnesty blocks the force of the new, the humility of asking forgiveness and the generosity of granting it. It perpetuates the misery of the old, the selfishness of those in power always reaping as much benefit as possible for themselves.

No society can survive without breaking with the evils of the past, without forgiveness and acceptance, above all after years of cruel war. Forgiveness, like truth, hurts but heals. So, we are not talking only in religious terms but also in social terms. Unless we reverse the sinful mechanisms we cannot build a new society. Thus the kind of amnesty granted, the date of its proclamation and the way in which it was done are not actions which reverse dehumanizing mechanisms but, sadly, ones which reinforce them.

### Disillusionment and the culture of inevitability

This amnesty tries to "amnesty" an entire social system, to hide from view the countless structural evils which have been inflicted on Salvadoreans for so long, not only by the military system, but by the economic, political, legal systems and the media. Given the speed with which the Assembly approved it, it might well also be interpreted as a kind of self-amnesty.

This amnesty discourages passing judgment on a whole system which plunged the country into death. It says "Don't bother about analysing, passing judgment and calling to account. If the military have come out of this unscathed, other invisible forces such as economic ones have nothing to fear". This confirms what the majority of the people strongly suspected: nothing good can be expected of the judiciary, because legality in its military, political, juridical, and economic forms always favours a few, to the detriment of the rest. To put it more bluntly, the poor feel that "illegality is their only salvation". Whether in seeking a livelihood in the U.S.A., or finding an imprisoned relative, or obtaining light and water, or getting a job, illegal channels have usually been more effective than legal ones.[5] This serious social evil, the almost total lack of confidence in the institutions, is adding strength to this amnesty.

Considering the other things that are happening in the country besides the amnesty, it is easy to understand the growing resignation, disillusionment and loss of hope. Both parties are responsible for this, though in different ways. The FMLN, which for some is an almost mythical alternative for a new society, also appears in the Report as answerable for criminal actions. Some of its leaders wanted to come to a secret agreement with Cristiani. The ghost of Sandinism in its degenerate and corrupt form may be hovering over our country.

People wonder whether the official system has any answer to offer the country, because the government is not doing enough or quickly enough to fulfil its promise to purge the army, set up a new national police force, grant land, and implement the recommendations of the Truth Commission. The Supreme Court does not accept blame for its negligence and irresponsible behaviour, nor does it offer any reparation. It simply hides itself behind its power and nationalistic demagogy. Needless to say, the Armed Forces neither acknowledge their dreadful crimes against the people nor seek forgiveness. Worse still, they distort the situation and appear offended, as if it were their good name and dignity that had been injured, and not that of the thousands of people murdered, tortured, disappeared at their hands, as the Report states. Thus they appear "unblemished" or "patriotic" and can retire without trial, without being called to account for their responsibilities – and with economic advantages.

Given all this, it is entirely understandable that many people wonder if everything in the country will not just go on as usual because it is always the same people who come out on top. They are asking whether it was worth all the suffering: whether there is a solution for this country, as those with the power keep legislating to make the rich richer and ignoring the poor.

This explains in part why people have not gone out into the streets en masse to protest against the amnesty and the non-implementation of the ad hoc commission and the Truth Commission.

The problem of resignation and disillusionment is all the more serious in that it is not only something local, arising from the immediate situation but is intrinsic in the new world order: hope has to be killed. As Xavier Gorostiaga has said, "The geopolitics of despair and the theology of inevitability today call for a global plan to make it easier to homogenize the new restructuring promoted by the global power elite. From the standpoint of the dominant, the attitude needed for stability is despair".[6] It seems that they want to inject a kind of postmodernity into the tragedy so that we accept that this is how things are, that there is not much sense in hoping for changes or struggling for them. They want to kill hope and introduce inevitability.

In Christian terms, while it would no longer be right to speak of a people crucified by violence, neither is there any vision of life and resurrection. We are still an impoverished people in danger of being cheated and plunged into disillusionment, condemned to the fatalism which its piety and its church have instilled for centuries. In the face of all this, the criticisms levelled against the leaders of the people by the prophets of the biblical Israel still ring true, because there is no sign of even the slightest change. And God's question to Cain still rings out: "Where is your brother?"

## 5. The stubbornness of hope

*Fifth proposition: The situation has changed and it is creating hope. But it has not changed to such an extent that we do not have to go on working and struggling. To keep change going on the right course, and to work and struggle for it, we have to create hope.*

### What does and does not encourage hope

Despite all that has been said above, there are also many very positive things connected with the Report. The mere fact of its having been made public and disseminated in different editions by the U.N., the FMLN, the ECA and the popular CIDEP edition (though the government did not publish it); the fact that it has the backing of the international community; that the FMLN, having been honest enough to accept responsibility for the acts attributed to it, has asked forgiveness and is ready to comply with the recommendations in its regard. Looking beyond the Report, it is a very positive fact – and one we hope will have far-reaching repercussions – that the war has not ended in a military victory for one side over another, but through negotiations, and that the cease-fire, demilitarization process and peace agreements have not been violated.

Still, while the scenario has changed, the structure of Salvadorean society has not. Salvadorean society, to put it mildly, has still not addressed itself to the suffering of the poor, whose situation must be changed because it is responsible for all the ills of the past. Although there is talk of small steps towards reconciliation, society is still structured adversarially. There is no real, substantial will to do anything significant to help the majority. The economic and social configuration does not serve the mass of the people. The conclusion is that the struggle must go on in the country, though not, of course, by war. This is necessary not only because no-one gives the poor anything, but because in the new scenario we find that the interests of those who hold power are taking precedence over the interests of the poor to an even greater extent. Indeed, they are working against the interests of the poor.

The changed scenario, therefore, does not call for reconciliation and convergence. It calls for continuing effort and struggle – an unmentionable word at present. But the new scenario has made some things easier, and it is to be hoped that it will do more. The struggle between truth and falsehood is clearly not over in the country, but for the first time the truth at least has the official backing of the Report in its favour.

### *The power of hope*

The new direction is well-defined in the peace agreements and the recommendations of the Truth Commission. But these set the direction for society in conceptual rather than practical terms. In the language used above, they have still not created tradition, they have still not become a physical path helping us to move forward.

How can we make the possibilities offered by the new scenario a historical reality?

The answer is complex, and all the forces for peace must work together in this task, each doing what it can. Hope is fundamental because it makes all the rest possible. Undoubtedly hope will have to be embodied but its central importance at this time is unquestionable. So let me say three things about how I understand this hope.

The first is that hope relates to utopia, not only to a possible future benefit. By utopia I mean that good which is still not real but which prompts human beings to act to make it so.

This utopia is neither a whim nor the product of an unfettered imagination. It is motivated by life itself. It consists first and foremost of life and of ridding the world of growing impoverishment and rising unemployment, both here and in the First World, the cruel result of the present economic development model. But powerful forces of evil – the anti-utopian forces – are actively working against it in this country and in the present world system. That being so, we have to understand hope as a real, historical force on the journey towards the utopia that has been described and in the struggle for it.

Secondly, we have to ask, who is the bearer of this hope? Theoretically the answer is obvious: the primary bearers of hope are those who suffer the present evils and long for the utopia – the masses of the people, the poor, the crucified people. Who can create hope and make it productive? Ideally, everyone ought to cooperate: the people themselves, organized with their social power, and the economic, political and – let us dream! – the military, who have the power to shape society. Historically the latter, to put it mildly, have created the opposite of hope.

The deepest and most difficult form of reconciliation is for those who have the power to place it at the service of those who have hope, and for those who have hope to turn society in the correct direction. Institutions with military, economic and political power are not by nature the primary bearers of either utopia or hope, while those who are indeed its bearers do not have power on their own to turn utopia and hope into historical realities. The essential step towards reconciliation is to resolve this paradox.

The third and last reflection is how to create hope, how to ensure that the popular majorities feel that life is truly possible, and how to achieve a collective conscience able to exert social pressure that may compel the different institutions to make the hopes of the majority into a historical reality. Believing this is possible is already an expression of hope, and others will have to analyse the practical political and economic conditions of that possibility. Here I shall concentrate on what seems to me to be the source of all hope, recalling briefly how hope and utopia have been created in this country. If I use Christian terms to do so, this is because both are central to faith, but also because today, it would seem that only theology has room for reflections of this kind. Elsewhere such thoughts are looked on with distrust and suspicion, if not scorn.

Hope and utopia have been created among us not as rational extrapolations or conclusions from one ideology or political activity or another, but as a product of dedication and commitment to the poor, and as a product of proclamation and of struggle for the truth which defends them, and of the risks they have run in facing their oppressors. Through all that, and I say this without false piety, the poor have grasped the fact that in this world there is compassion and love, which right up to the present day, from Jesus of Nazareth to Monsignor Romero, creates and sustains hope.

Many things remain to be done, chief among them being to uphold or restore hope for the popular majorities. By hope, I mean the force – personal but also social – to attain, on the way towards utopia, the minimum requirements of decent, just and fraternal life.

Don Pedro Casaldáliga recently said, "many things, including life and liberty, may be lost to us. But if we lose hope, we lose everything".

Does such hope exist in El Salvador? Is it present in the collective conscience of the majorities as a shared hope? This is one of the most important questions today – perhaps the most important. There certainly has been hope, and it has produced many good things. Perhaps some are now trying to make hope disappear – or at least deprive it of its former strength by reducing it to moderate optimism which could at best stimulate reconciliation, tolerance, forgetting, pragmatism, realism, etc. Hope and moderate optimism are not in opposition. Both are necessary. They must complement each other and the one must not be substituted in arbitrary fashion for the other. But they are not the same, and if hope disappears all the other realities will lose their specific good for us. Consequently, upholding hope in this country is very important. Would that those whose duty it is to turn it into a historical reality, and who have the power to do so, uphold hope. But those who can generate hope are the peoples' organization, the trade unions, educational centres, universities and churches.

We have already seen the importance of the Report of the Truth Commission, and its roots in that which is best in the Salvadorean people. The Report has produced hope, but what is done with it can produce more hope or new despair. If the Report is ignored, distorted or diluted in nefarious ways, as the military and the authorities wish, or even in the "reasonable ways" to which politicians usually appeal, that will be an immeasurable evil for the country. It will strip it of its hope.

## NOTES

1. The same thing would happen if other institutions were to analyse the truth of the economy, the administration of justice, the media: they would show a country turned inside out or upside down.
2. To use the language of "idolatry" used by Monsignor Romero supported in this by I. Ellacuría, the dynamic of violence begins with the idolizing of money, "the absolutizing of wealth and private property". This in turn calls for "the absolutizing of national security", i.e. of the Armed Forces, the paramilitaries and the death squads – all in order to maintain the initial idolatry. Finally, what usually happens in response is that the people organize, with the resulting violence, all of which can also lead to "the absolutizing of organization", i.e. to its idolization. Thus, the Report can be analysed in a way that is no less true and useful for being intuitive and simple, in terms of idolatry and absolutizing, as condemning the second and third idolatries, but without mentioning the first which leads to all the others (which was not its task). For Monsignor Romero's thinking on idolatry, see J. Sobrino, I. Martín Baró and R. Cardenal, *La voz de los sin voz. La palabra viva de Monsignor Romero* (San Salvador, 1981) 145ff.
3. By way of example, it will suffice to recall the statements of Monsignor Romeo Tovar Astorga, who accused the FMLN of responsibility for the UCA murders, and recently attacked the Report of the Truth Commission, defending the system of justice which the Report recommends should be purged.
4. In my view this attitude of Cristiani's also discourages hope because, assuming he wants to comply with the spirit and letter of the Report, he cannot act against the Armed Forces, who have the balance of power in their favour as never before – many internal forces and above all the most powerful foreign elements, notably the USA, the United Nations Security Council and the European Community. Hence many people wonder what will happen in the country when international pressure and the presence of the UN Observer Mission in El Salvador (ONUSAL) decreases.
5. Sects have solved the problem more radically still: there is no salvation in the things of earth, so we must trust to the things of heaven.
6. X. Gorostiaga, "La mediación de las ciencias sociales y los cambios internacionales", in J. Comblin, J. I. Gonzaléz Faus, J. Sobrino, *Cambio social y pensamiento cristiano en América Latina*, Madrid, 1992, p.113

# BIBLIOGRAPHY

**Never Again! series.** A number of significant publications have appeared in Latin America on the nature and scale of military repression which occurred since 1970. One might refer to them as being in that category of "Never Again!" books: Some were initiatives taken by newly elected governments which set up commissions to investigate human rights violations since 1976. Others came about as a result of intense work by human rights groups, ecumenical groups, churches and other non-governmental bodies to make known the truth as a first step in achieving justice. Often at considerable risk these groups dug out, collated and published full accounts of the offences incurred, drawing upon public records, restricted material and testimonies. They sought as much as possible to identify offenders by name.

Readers are encouraged to examine such publications, a sample of which are listed below. They have become authoritative reference points in the countries where they have appeared. They are listed in the chronological order of their appearance.

*1. Donde Están? Tomos I a VII.* Santiago de Chile: Vicaría de la Solidaridad del Arzobispado de Santiago, 1978.

*2. Desaparecidos en la Argentina/Disappeared in Argentina* (Spanish/English). The list of disappeared published by the *Comité de Defensa de Derechos Humanos en el Cono Sur (CLAMOR).* São Paulo, Brazil: Archdiocese of São Paulo, 1982.

*3. Nunca Más: The Report of the Argentine National Commission on the Disappeared.* New York: Farrar Straus Giroux, 1986. First published in Great Britain by Faber and Faber Ltd.: 1986. Originally published in Spanish under the title *Nunca Más: Informe de la Comisión Nacional Sobre la Desaparición de Personas,* with a supplementary book, *Anexos.* Buenos Aires: Editorial Universitária de Buenos Aires, 1984.

*4. Brasil: Nunca Mais: Um Relato para a História.* Prefaces by the Cardinal-Archbishop of São Paulo, Paulo Evaristo Arns, and by the General Secretary of the WCC, Philip Potter. Petrópolis: Editora Vozes, 1985. Published in English under the title of *Torture in Brazil: A Report by the Archdiocese of São Paulo.* (Edited by Dassin, J.; translator: Wright, J.). New York: Vintage Books (Random House), 1986.

5. *Projeto: Brasil Nunca Mais,* a 6891-page, twelve-volume record of repression under military rule in Brazil, under the titles: *Tomo I: O Regime Militar; Tomo II, Vol. 1: A Pesquisa; Vol. 2: Os Atingidos; Vol. 3: Os Funcionários; Tomo III: Perfil dos Atingidos* (also published separately by Vozes, 1988); *Tomo IV: As Leis Repressivas; Tomo V, Vol. 1: A Tortura; Vol. 2: As Torturas; Vol. 3: As Torturas; Vol. 4: Os Mortos; Tomo VI, Vol. 1: Indices dos Anexos; Vol. 2: Inventário dos Anexos.* São Paulo: Archdiocese of São Paulo, 1985.

6. *El Diario del Juicio: Porque la História es el Prólogo del Mundo que Heredaran Nuestros Hijos. Tomos I y II.* Buenos Aires: Editorial Perfil, 1985. The complete collection of *verbatim* testimonies of witnesses at the trial of military officers in Buenos Aires.

7. *Assassinatos no Campo: Crime e Impunidade, 1964-1986.* Prepared by the *Movimento dos Trabalhadores Rurais Sem Terra.* São Paulo: Global editora, 1987.

8. *Uruguay: Nunca Más: Informe sobre la Violación a los Derechos Humanos (1972-1985).* Montevideo: Servicio Paz y Justicia, 1989.

9. *Chile: La Memoria Prohibida: Las Violaciones a los Derechos Humanos, 1973-1983. Tomos I-III.* Authors: Atria, R.; Egaña, J.L.; Góngora, A.; Quesney, C.; Saball, G.; Villalobos, G. Santiago de Chile: Pehuén Editores, 1989.

10. *Report of the Chilean National Commission on Truth and Reconciliation, Volumes I and II.* Notre Dame, Indiana: Notre Dame Law School, 1993. Originally published in Spanish under the title *Chile. Informe Rettig: Informe de la Comisión Nacional de Verdad y Reconciliación, Tomos I y II.* Santiago de Chile: La Nación, 1991. Summary French edition under *Synthèse du Rapport de la Commission Vérité et Réconciliation.* Santiago de Chile: Commission Chilienne des Droits de l'Homme et Centre IDEAS, 1991.

11. *El Precio de la Paz ( Paraguay).* Authors: Blanch, J.M.; Acuña, E.; Bareiro, L.; Borda, D.; Elías, R.; Irigoitia, A.; Munárriz, J.M.; Prieto, E.; Valiente, H.; Weyer, G.; Yore, M. Asunción: Centro de Estudios Paraguayos "Antonio Guasch" (CEPAG), 1991.

12. *Série Nunca Más* (Paraguay): Vol. I: *La Dictadura de Stroessner y los Derechos Humanos.* Author: Simon G., J.L.; Vol. II & III: *Testimonios de la Represión Política en Paraguay 1975-1989.* Author: Alcala, G.R. Asunción: Comité de Iglesias, 1992/93.

13. *El Terrorismo de Estado en Colombia.* Bruselas: published by the *Nationaal Centrum voor Ontwikkelingssamenwerking (NCOS),* 1992. And *Tras los Pasos Perdidos de la Guerra Sucia: Paramilitarismo*

*y Operaciones encubiertas en Colombia*. Both volumes were published in cooperation with Columbian human rights entities and under the auspices of ten international non-governmental organizations. Bruselas: Ediciones NCOS, 1995.

*14. Votre Cri Ne Sera Pas Etouffé*. Etudes et rapports sur les violations des droits humains en Haiti. Genève: Edité par le Centre Haïtien de Recherches et de Documentation (CHRD), la Commission tiers-monde de l'Eglise catholique (COTMEC), et Haïti-Informations, 1993.

*15. Justicia y Dignidad: Alegato Presentado por la Parte Civil Acusadora en el Juicio de Responsabilidades Contra la Dictadura de García Meza*. Plaintifs: Ivan Paz Claros, I.; Trigo de Quiroga Santa Cruz, C.; Salas Moya, O.; Ríos Araoz, M. Authors: Del Granado Cosio, J.; Padilla Ledezma, F.; Sandoval, J.C.; Virrueta, M.A.; Gutierrez Sardan, J.L. on behalf of the *Asamblea de Derechos Humanos de Bolivia, the Central Obrera Boliviana, the Sistema Nacional Universitário and the Familiares de las Víctimas de la Dictadura*. Sucre: Talleres Gráficos, 1992. And *Juicio de Responsabilidad: Sentencia Histórica Contra La Impunidad*. Sucre: Ediciónes Gráficas "E.G.", 1993.

*16. "From Madness to Hope, the Report of the Commission on the Truth for El Salvador", published in The United Nations and El Salvador, 1990-1995, Blue Books Series, Volume IV.* New York: Department of Public Information, United Nations, 1995.

*17. Boletín de la Coordenadora Nacional de Derechos Humanos del Perú (CNDHP)*: a collection of monthly reports published from 1990 to 1992 by the coordinating body of forty-seven national human rights entities and movements. Also published by the CNDHP: *Los Sucesos del Alto Huallaga*, Lima:1994, and *El Nombre de los Inocentes*, Lima: 1995.

*18. Los Inocentes Tienen Nombre: 300 Histórias de Prisión Injusta en el Perú*. Published by a collective of five human rights entities: APRODEH, COMISEDH, CEAPAZ, FEDEPAZ, CEAPAZ, and IDEELE. Lima: 1995.

**Additional publications on impunity** and on ethical dimensions regarding reconciliation and human rights have been found to be of value and use. Some of them are listed here.

*19.* A number of small booklets containing the articles of the UN Universal Declaration of Human Rights, each one annotated with biblical texts and church statements, have been published since the early 1970s for pedagogical use in churches and movements. Beginning with a first edition of over a million copies in Portuguese, published by the Brazilian ecumenical agency CESE, new editions subsequently appeared in Spanish, French, Creole, Guarani and English published by ecumenical entities, among other countries, in Argentina, Chile, Switzerland, Haiti, Paraguay and Canada.

Some **important symposia and conferences** on impunity have been organized by Latin American national, regional and related international entities. Some principle publications containing reports and contributions made, as well as conclusions reached, are contained in the following books:

*20. Le refus de l'oubli: la politique de disparition forcée de personnes.* Colloquium of Paris, January-February 1981. Paris: Berger-Levrault, 1982.

*21. La desaparición: crimen contra la humanidad.* Faculty of Law and Social Sciences of the National University of Buenos Aires, 24-25 March 1987. Published by the Asamblea Permanente por los Derechos Humanos (Permanent Assembly for Human Rights), Buenos Aires: 1987.

*22. La desaparición forzada como crimen de la lesa humanidad: Instrumentos juridicos internacionales para la prevención y contra la impunidad.* Organized by the *Grupo de Iniciativa* (sixteen Argentinian human rights entities) at the Colloquium of Buenos Aires, 10-13 October 1988. Buenos Aires: Paz Producciones, 1989.

*23. No a la impunidad. Los Familiares no callaran!* Ninth Congress of FEDEFAM (The Latin American Federation of Associations of the Relatives of the Disappeared), 26 November-2 December 1989, Lima, Peru. Caracas: Talleres Gráficos Acción Ecumenica, 1990.

*24. Proceso a la impunidad de crimenes de lesa humanidad en América latina 1989-1991.* Tribunal Permanente de los Pueblos: Liga International por los Derechos y la Liberación de los Pueblos, Sección Colombiana. Bogotá: 1991.

*25. Justice, Not Impunity: Impunity of Perpetrators of Gross Human Rights Violations.* An International Meeting organized by the *Commission nationale consultative des droits de l'homme* and the International Commission of Jurists, under the auspices of the United Nations, 2-5 November 1992. Geneva: ICJ, 1993. Spanish edition: *Nó a la Impunidad, Sí a la Justicia: la impunidad de los autores de violaciones graves a los derechos humanos. Encuentro International, Ginebra: CIJ, 1993.* French edition: *Non à l'impunité, Oui à la justice:* L'impunité des auteurs de violations graves des droits de l'homme. Rencontre Internationales. Genève: CIJ, 1993.

26. *Solidarités et Responsabilités Face à la Torture.* Proceedings of the Colloquium of Strasbourg, 2-3 September 1994. Organized by the Action of Christians for the Abolition of Torture (ACAT - France). Paris: 1995.

27. A related study on the effects of torture is contained in *Trauma, Duelo y Reparación: una experiencia de trabajo psicosocial en Chile.* Published by FASIC, Santiago: Editorial interamericana, 1987.

# CONTRIBUTORS

**José Burneo** is a lawyer and the first director of the Ecumenical Foundation for Development and Peace (FEDEPAZ), a human rights organization based in Lima, Peru.

**Rafael Goto** is a journalist, pastor of the Evangelical Church of the Pilgrims, and general coordinator of the Christian Centre for Development and Services (CEPS), in Lima, Peru.

**Guillermo Kerber** is a Roman Catholic theologian and the director of Ecumenical Service for Human Dignity (SEDHU), based in Montevideo, Uruguay.

**Luis Pérez Aguirre**, a Jesuit priest, founded the Uruguayan human rights organization Peace and Justice Service (SERPAJ), and at present leads the *Misión de Fé y Solidaridad,* based in Montevideo, Uruguay.

**Aracelli Ezzatti de Rocchietti**, a Methodist educator, is a prison chaplain in Montevideo, Uruguay.

**Carlos Delmonte** is a pastor of the Waldensian Church in Uruguay.

**Ademar Olivera**, works in the barrios of Montevideo as a pastor of the Malvin Methodist Parish.

**Raul Soza** is a pastor serving parishes of the Methodist Evangelical Church in Argentina, in Trelew and Puerto Madryn.

**Paz Rojas Baeza** is a Chilean neuro-psychiatric physician, who coordinates the mental health team of the Committee of the Defence of People's Rights (CODEPU), in Santiago, Chile.

**The Ecumenical Coordinating Assembly** is made up of lay persons and pastors of the Protestant and Catholic communities in Chile.

**Dagoberto Ramírez F.** is professor of Holy Scriptures in the Evangelical Theological Community and is a member of the board of the Evangelical Service Corporation for Development (SEPADE).

**Héctor Salazar Ardiles** is a jurist who, served on the legal teams of the Committee for Peace, the Vicariate of Solidarity of the Roman Catholic Church, and is at present with the Social Assistance Foundation of the Christian Churches (FASIC), in Santiago, Chile.

**The Permanent Assembly for Human Rights of Bolivia** is a coalition of representatives of labour unions, the Association of

Relatives of Detainees and the Disappeared, Roman Catholic and Protestant evangelical churches, religious orders, university students, workers and journalists, with chapters throughout the country.

**Jon Sobrino** is a Jesuit theologian and is Professor of Philosophy and Theology at the University of Central America (UCA) in San Salvador, El Salvador.

**Charles Harper** (Editor), a Presbyterian clergyman, was director of WCC's Human Rights Resources Office for Latin America from 1974 to 1992.

**Dwain C. Epps** is coordinator of International Affairs (CCIA) in the WCC.